THE ROAD EAST

THE ROAD EAST

AMERICA'S NEW DISCOVERY OF EASTERN WISDOM

HARRISON POPE, JR.

BEACON PRESS   BOSTON

Copyright © 1974 by Harrison Pope, Jr.

Beacon Press books are published under the auspices of the Unitarian
Universalist Association

Published simultaneously in hardcover and paperback editions

Simultaneous publication in Canada by Saunders of Toronto, Ltd.

9 8 7 6 5 4 3 2 1

Library of Congress Cataloging in Publication Data

Pope, Harrison.
    The road East.
    Bibliography: p. 150.
    1. East – Religion.   2. Youth – Religious life.
I. Title.
BL1032.P6   181'.1   73-16887
ISBN 0-8070-1126-6
ISBN 0-8070-1127-4 (pbk.

CONTENTS

1. The Road East   1

2. The Digestion of the Drug Culture   21

3. Poison and Purification   38

4. From the Fillmore to the Farm   54

5. Anxiety, Adulthood, Old Age, and Death   67

6. Guilt, Aggression, and the Righteousness Game   88

7. Science, Sanity, Madness, and Magic   104

8. Searching for the Sphere   124

9. The Transformation of the Self   135

Afterword: The Methods Used in this Study   140

Reference Notes   144

Bibliography   150

Index   155

ACKNOWLEDGMENTS

The idea of this book first began to grow in my mind in early 1972, when I started a study of the American youth "counterculture." For help in this period I especially thank my advisor, Dr. Jane Murphy, at the Harvard School of Public Health. I am also very grateful to the Cambridge branch of the Students' International Meditation Society and to Erewhon Trading Post for their unfailing and good-natured assistance with my two small quantitative studies.

But my greatest appreciation goes to the many people who introduced me to the different Eastern disciplines, particularly Jeff Strnad, Richard Margolin, Charles Allan, and Walter Van Vort. Each of them has been involved in a different sector of the Eastern subculture (Transcendental Meditation, Gurdjieff, Guru Maharaj Ji, Krishna, and Tai Chi) and each has helped me with the actual manuscript and with the reference notes. In addition, I warmly thank many other friends, including Lorne Ouellet, Larry Cross, Timothy O'Brien, Don Leopold, Adrian, Jerry, Susan, Keith, and Martha, all of whom appear in the quotations and anecdotes of this book. Though I have altered their stories slightly so as not to make them recognizable to outsiders, they will have no trouble recognizing themselves, under various pseudonyms. I hope that I have done justice to all of them and preserved the essence, if not the exact words, of their accounts and conversations.

Finally, I thank the innumerable other youths whom I met in passing along the road East. They not only taught me much about the East, but caused me to reconsider many of my own beliefs about science and Western society. For this, for their friendship, and for the good times we shared, I shall always remember them.

THE ROAD EAST

1/THE ROAD EAST

A QUIET REVOLUTION

It is a warm Thanksgiving weekend at a grand old resort hotel on Cape May. Two hundred Transcendental Meditators have assembled there for a "residence course" — a weekend of meditation, yoga asanas, and lectures. After Friday dinner, groups of meditators are clustering into the ballroom-turned-lecture-hall.

Tonight's lecture is about the higher states of consciousness. A white-robed teacher of meditation, one of Maharishi's close disciples, begins to speak:

> "Now as we all know, there are three ordinary states of consciousness: waking, sleeping, and dreaming. Each of these is pretty much distinct from the others. We don't have too much trouble agreeing on which one is which. And after those three, the fourth state is transcendental consciousness, which we experience in meditation. I'm sure you've all heard a good deal about transcendental consciousness. So now, onward to five, six, and seven!"

He walks over to a blackboard and draws two vertical lines, dividing it into three columns. He labels them, "5: Cosmic Consciousness," "6: 'God' Consciousness," and "7: Unity Consciousness."

Then he begins a long discussion, gradually adding words and phrases under each of the three headings, and periodically turning to the audience to emphasize a distinction. At one point, he says,

> "So now in the fifth state, once we have attained pure, unbounded awareness we become capable of seeing all the way down to the finest relative values of the object. Now a mind which is unable to perceive these

1

finest levels sees only the surface value of the object. So as a result such a mind sees only the qualities of the object which distinguish it from other objects in the environment, and therefore, the boundaries of the object appear to be rigidly defined. The mind which has attained cosmic consciousness comes to see beyond those boundaries."

Twenty minutes later, having nearly filled the board, he continues,

"So, to put it in a different way, the question we are asking in reference to the seventh state of consciousness is whether or not it is possible to experience, on a cognitive level, the transcendental absolute that lies beyond the subtlest level of the relative. You understand? But you see, perception cannot achieve this so long as perception involves an object of perception in addition to a perceiver, since the absolute is unmanifest, and therefore, by definition, unperceivable, yes?

"However — and this is the point — once we have reached that sixth state of consciousness, and become aware of the most subtle levels of the relative world, the finest levels of the relative, then the unbounded, unmanifest value which exists within the finest level of the relative becomes *lively*! And that liveliness which the mind comes to perceive in the object, or I should say, in the transcendental essence of all objectivity, is nothing more or less than *itself*, the liveliness of the mind's own pure, unbounded awareness. So that when the seventh state is achieved, the subject-object dichotomy is gone! Knowledge has crossed the gap that separates the knower from the known!"

As he goes on to summarize his explanations, he writes at the bottom of the three columns: "I am That," "All This is That," and "That alone Is."

"Now a lot of this has been very technical," he concludes. "And if you don't understand it, that's perfectly all right, because understanding it intellectually is really beside the point. It's something which we must ultimately *experience* through our daily practice of meditation." He smiles. "This is just to whet your ap-

petite, to give you a little taste of what lies up ahead.
But you don't have to understand a single word of this lecture in order to actually *understand.* All you have to do is
keep meditating regularly! Any questions?"

After a long pause, a boy with an enormous red beard sheepishly
raises his hand:

"I'm sorry, but I guess I lost you. I just got all confused
about half way through."

"Yeah, so did I," says another. "Can you say it again
more simply?" We all murmur in agreement.

"I am sorry," he replies. "I think that I became too
complicated, too abstruse, in talking about all this. But
you must remember, intellectual understanding is only
secondary. It's not important. So let me try to simplify
it for you."

He picks up an eraser and begins to remove various portions of what
he has written on the blackboard, pausing occasionally, then deciding
to erase some more. Eventually, having erased more than two-thirds
of what he has written, he turns back to the audience. "All right. Now
. . . but wait a minute. I'm *still* being too complicated."

Again he starts with the eraser. After a moment, he is about to turn
back to the audience, but then, reconsidering, he erases still more, until
only the three phrases at the bottom remain: "I am That," "All This
is That," and "That alone Is."

"There! *Now*," he begins. But then a sly smile steals across his face.
Turning back to the board, he briskly erases everything but the final
"Is." "There, I have at last simplified it!" he begins to chuckle. "And
I have answered your question, too, yes? Heh, heh, heh!" An instant's
silence, and suddenly everyone starts laughing.

•   •   •

For nearly an hour before the doors of the hall are to open, the followers of the Guru Maharaj Ji are fully assembled. Smiling, neatly
dressed, they cluster on the steps of Harvard's Lowell Lecture Hall,
waiting to hear Rennie Davis, the former radical leader, who is now
touring the country to proselytize for the fifteen-year-old master.

This visit will be no ordinary whistle stop, however, because Cambridge is home to more radical activists than any community except
Berkeley, California. In the minds of movement stalwarts, Rennie's

religious conversion is more than folly; it is betrayal. In Berkeley a week earlier, the angry audience pelted Davis with tomatoes. The question to be answered: will Cambridge be more civil — or less?

When the doors open, the guru's devotees spread themselves evenly throughout the auditorium. Slowly the hall fills as the hostile forces arrive. Tension mounts as dark mutterings and wisecracks grow louder.

A bearded young man walks on stage with a guitar and stands before the microphone. Behind him is an empty throne covered with white satin and surrounded by fresh bouquets. Above it is a portrait of the chubby guru. Speaking very softly, he says that he will precede Davis with a song, "Who is Maharaj Ji?" He begs the audience to relax, open their minds, "to just *check it out.*"

The loyal forces join him in singing and applaud wildly at the end. They are joined by a chorus of boos as Rennie Davis approaches the mike.

Davis waits silently for order, his hands clasped loosely before him. Finally, smiling, he says, "No one is more aware than me how outrageous this is." Somewhat disarmed, the audience laughs.

Speaking in carefully measured phrases, he reiterates the soft-sell "check it out" theme, then explains how he became involved. He was on a flight to Paris, he says, to celebrate the Vietnam cease-fire with Madame Binh when he ran into a friend who offered him a ticket to Prem Nagar, the guru's headquarters in India. He accepted it. At first, he confessed, he was sickened by the antics of this child divinity who loves motorbikes. But enlightenment came one day on the way to do his laundry. He found himself suddenly attacked by a swarm of ravens. Pulling out a pillow case to fend them off, he found it embroidered with the words "Lord of the Universe." The birds flew away at once and suddenly Rennie *knew.* "Now," he says, "I would crawl across the planet to kiss his toes."

"All I know, brothers and sisters, is that it happened and it's happening now. We're experiencing a love story.

"When the Guru Maharaj Ji enlightens you, he gives you *direct knowledge*, knowledge that you can feel. It's the realest rush you'll ever feel. It's pure energy."

He pauses. "You know, I used to be like most people, I felt the most energy in the mornings, but as the day wore on, I became more and more tired. Now —"

In the rear a radical turns to his buddy, "No shit, when
Rennie stayed in my apartment he started smoking hash
as soon as he woke up. He would go through two grams
by noon. No wonder!"

"Now," Davis continues, "my lowest point of the day is when
I get up. As the day goes by, I just get more and more energy.
By night, I'm so high I can barely get to sleep!"

Suddenly a shabby, long-haired young man bounds onstage and plops
on the satin throne. A gasp rises from the followers, a roar of laughter
from the skeptics. Rennie stands quietly as the freak, a former Harvard student, parodies the gestures of a monarch, blowing kisses to the
crowd and grinning absurdly. Several men in suits try vainly to persuade the intruder to leave. Then they depart to summon police. As
they return with a Harvard cop, the boy on the throne quickly vanishes
via a rear exit.

"People, you're in for a big surprise," Davis calmly re-
sumes. "Everything we've dreamed of for years can come
true. All the goals of the movement — an end to war, poverty, racism, sexism, nationalism — will be achieved. And we're
not talking about just sometime within our lifetime; we're
talking about five, ten years from now. Fifteen years *at the
latest*!"

"The Maharaj Ji eats scab lettuce!" shouts a heckler.

Ignoring him, Davis continues. "When you surrender to
Guru Maharaj Ji's love, it changes your whole nervous system, your whole body chemistry. You've all heard of the
third eye, the pineal gland, right? Science doesn't understand it. Well, when you receive knowledge from this Master, you begin to see with your third eye. You hear celes-
tial music. And you begin to taste a sweet fluid, a sort of
divine honey.

"Activation of the pineal gland," he says, tapping his
forehead, "is the key to controlling aggression. In fact, aggression just drops away. When you realize that you are
pure conscious energy, you realize that everything's possible.

Rennie then describes "Soul Rush '73," a global rally to be held November 1973 in the Houston Astrodome. He promises an historic event.

"Everything's gonna come together at last. Millions will attend. There will be exhibits covering the entire history of religious thought. Pavilions devoted to the great teachers from Moses to Buddha, and to the occult mysteries. Everything will all be explained: the lost continent of Atlantis, the Incas, magic, numerology. Tarot, astrology, ESP, everything. We're gonna put it all in perspective."

He introduces the film that will follow, showing the guru at a rally in India attended by a million people. Then with the words "Jai Satchitanand!" he exits. The faithful echo him, "Jai Satchitanand!"

Much of the audience begins leaving during the film, which features — to the delight of the followers — baby pictures of the guru. Outside, a cluster of radical luminaries begin an animated *post mortem* conversation.

"Too much acid!"

"No, I think he is sincere, but it's still an ego trip for him. He's still on stage."

"He *is* articulate as hell, you know," says a third, shaking his head. "He knows how to raise hopes, to suggest that we're on the brink of something *big.* Just like Mayday."

States another, in a matter-of-fact tone: "The whole appeal of the Maharaj Ji is his youth. So you can dream of everything. It gives the imagination free rein."

"Rennie's more poised, you must admit," someone suggests.

"Yeah, but did you notice that his fingernails are still bitten down to the quick?"

All over Cambridge, the conversations continue into the night.

•   •   •

It is six o'clock in the morning in Palo Alto, California. A lean, blond college girl jumps out of bed, pulls off her nightgown, and walks nude into the living room, where sunlight is just beginning to touch the leaves of the flowers under the windows. Facing East, she kneels, back straight, and sits with eyes closed for several minutes. Then, looking straight into the sun, she begins a series of postures, smoothly as a ballet dancer: standing upright with hands together, then touching her toes, then stretching on the floor as though she were doing pushups. But the exercises do not look remotely like Western pushups. They are too relaxed, too unstrained, as if no effort were being expended in their execution. There is something refreshingly noncompetitive about them; even the most vigorous motions seem calm and gentle.

The postures continue in a smooth progression for ten minutes, each repeated one or two times. At the end, she silently returns to the original sitting pose and again closes her eyes. Blocking off her left nostril with two fingers of one hand, she takes a slow breath, then repeats the process while blocking the other nostril with her thumb. The breathing exercise — pranayama — lasts for about twelve minutes. Near the end, she is breathing only once every sixteen seconds.

*   *   *

In Miami, Florida, a nineteen-year-old boy tells this story:

"Well, me and my friend Steve used to turn on all the time together. That's all we ever did was smoke dope and get high. And so last summer I came back from college and went and found him in the store where he was working in Miami and I said, 'Hey, man, let's turn on!' but he said, 'No, man, I'm not doing grass anymore. I'm into Baba!' I said, 'Baba?' and he said, 'Yeah, man. It's really beautiful. It's the most beautiful thing I've ever been into. You've got to come with me and go to a Baba meeting!' So all afternoon he was telling me about Meher Baba, and he showed me these books that Baba had written and everything.

"So that night we went to this meeting. And the first thing that happened was that this girl I had never seen came up to me and threw her arms around me and said, 'Jai Baba!' which means sort of like, 'Hail, Baba' or something like that. And that really blew my mind, to just have this girl come up and throw her arms around me. So as this meeting went on I got the feeling that there was all this *energy* in the air, all this positive energy, all this aliveness. It was really beautiful, and I started getting turned on to it. You see, at a meeting you don't have to pray or do any rituals, or meditate, or anything like that. All you have to do is love Baba! And it's all joyous! And after awhile I started going around and throwing my arms around people and saying 'Jai Baba!' too.

"Then this girl who had just come back from India got

up and talked, and when she spoke it was really beautiful.
She talked about going to Baba's tomb, and when she walked inside, suddenly this incredible sadness came over her and
she started to cry. And there was this guy with her, and he
was really skeptical, so he didn't cry. But when he stepped
outside the tomb again, it suddenly hit him and he broke
down and cried and came back to her and said, 'Oh,
wow. Now I know what you mean!'

"So after I came out from that meeting, I had already
fallen in love with Baba. I said, 'Gee, if Baba can give all
this joy and all this energy to all these people then I want
to love Baba!' So after that I started going to Baba meetings very time I could, and I've been down to the commune in South Carolina. There are people there who
actually knew Baba, who actually were with him, and
they're really beautiful to talk to. So it's been two years
now since I first got turned on to Baba, and it's getting
more and more beautiful all the time."

· · ·

In an apartment in the heart of Manhattan, sixty youths gather for
the evening meeting of Nicherin Shoshu. Facing the Gohonzon, a little
cabinet with Oriental characters written inside, they begin to chant:
"Nam-myoho-renge-kyo, Nam-myoho-renge-kyo." The monotone of
their voices coalesces into a solid sound; the entire room resonates as
though it were being activated by a single giant voice. A series of other
chants follows, then a brief talk by the leader, and finally another
fifteen-minute round of Nam-myoho-renge-kyo. As the service draws
to an end, the previously sober faces begin to light up with exuberance.
Suddenly, as if set off by a signal, the entire male contingent of the
group leaps to its feet, right fists extended into the air, singing a rous-
ing Nicherin Shoshu song, punctuated with cheers and claps from the
girls. The instant that the boys sit down, the girls leap up with their
song, with zest and choreography that would match a Broadway musi-
cal. Another, longer cheer at the end, and one of the boys in front
jumps up:

"Who wants to tell about experiences?"

"I do! I do!" screams a girl. She bounds to the front of
the audience.

"I want to tell everybody that it's really true! You really *do* get what you chant for with your *Gohonzon.* I've had my *Gohonzon* for only two months now, and it's just wonderful! I had always hoped that I could find someone who would teach me Spanish, so I chanted for that. And today in school I met a girl from Columbia who wants to teach me Spanish! Isn't that great?"

She giggles with glee, receives another cheer from the crowd and bounces back to her seat.

"More experiences! Who has another experience?" says the boy.

"I do!" says a blond teenager. Everyone becomes quieter; apparently he is one of the more influential experience-tellers.

"My sister was in a car accident last week, and I've chanted all week for her to have a fast recovery in the hospital. She got out of the hospital today. She's still limping but she was really surprised at how fast she recovered, and so were the doctors. I guess they thought she'd be in the hospital for months. But they didn't know about what the Gohonzon could do!"

More experiences follow. Three visitors coming to their first meeting are introduced, and a question period follows. One of the visitors, a girl in her early twenties, asks,

"How can everybody be so happy and bouncy all the time? It seems almost, almost . . ."

The leader grins. "Corny you mean?"

"Well, yes."

"Just try it for awhile. Try chanting, and see what happens.

"Well, maybe I will."

At the end of the meeting, the group locks arms in a giant circle for another round of animated Nicherin Shoshu songs, followed by further cheers.

•　•　•

A young girl, a member of an Ananda Marga commune, answers the questions of a skeptical outsider in San Francisco:

"But what do you actually *do* when you meditate? I

mean, is there really any difference between what you do and what I do when I'm just sitting on my bed thinking about something?"

"Oh, yes, Ananda Marga is an actual technique. It's a very specific method for drawing the mind toward higher levels of awareness."

"You have to concentrate on something? I mean, do you stare at your navel or something?"

"No. In fact to concentrate would actually be a mistake. It would draw you away from where you are going, rather than towards it."

"So instead you just sit and let your mind drift off into the clouds, and get sort of spaced out?"

"Oh, no. As I said before it's a very concrete technique. You get taught how to do it by a teacher of Ananda Marga."

"Does it take a long time to learn how to do it right?"

"A few minutes."

"A few minutes? That's all? And then you know the whole thing? Isn't there anything else?"

"Well, after you've meditated for a certain period of months, you can go on to a more sophisticated technique. There are several higher levels of technique, as you become more advanced."

"How much do you have to pay to get this few minutes of instruction?"

"It's free. There's no charge."

"Really? Well, then why don't you show me how to do it?"

"No, that would be bad. In order to preserve the purity of the teaching, it is important that you be taught by an actual teacher who has learned to impart the knowledge to others."

"Oh. Well, after you learn how to do it, do you just meditate any time you feel like it?"

"No. Twice a day, in the morning and the evening."

"So what happens to you? I mean where do you get after you've meditated for fifty years? Does your brain gradually turn into marshmallow? Is it like the equivalent of a frontal lobotomy, maybe? What do you actually *experience,* anyhow?"

"Bliss."

"Bliss?"

"Yes, *Ananda Marga* means 'The way of bliss' "

"Well, what's the difference between that bliss and the bliss I feel when I've had six beers? Or is it like getting high with marijuana?"

"I think you'd be surprised at how rapidly you would lose interest in alcohol or marijuana after you started meditating. Or even those cigarettes you're smoking. I know of one guy who was an alcoholic before he started Ananda Marga. He drank about a quart of gin a day and usually a bottle of wine besides. Within about a month after he started meditating he had completely stopped drinking, and he hasn't touched it since."

"It sounds to me more like some kind of psychotherapy than a religion."

"Well, it's much more than psychotherapy, but it isn't really a religion, that's true."

"Do you believe in God?"

"That depends on what you mean by 'God,' but in the terms that I think you mean by 'God' the answer is no. It's not that sort of thing at all. But in another sense you may realize God to a degree that you never have before, as you advance in meditation."

•   •   •

Transcendental Meditation, Guru Maharaj Ji, Meher Baba, Ananda Marga, Nicherin Shoshu, Hatha Yoga: these are only a few of the many Eastern schools which have risen to prominence during the last few years in the United States. In any major city in the country, for example, one can now learn half a dozen different forms of Yoga alone, some taught by itinerant Indian teachers, but most taught by young Americans who wish to spread the doctrine to a wider group. Nicherin Shoshu and Zen are only two of several sects of Buddhism in America; Tibetan Buddhism, for example, a technique as different from the first two as they are from each other, now has chapters in most cities and two sizable communes which offer courses and retreats for outsiders. Guru Maharaj Ji is one of a score of Eastern masters who have accumulated a following in the United States. Many of the older gurus, including ones who left their physical bodies long ago ("died," in our terminology) have been suddenly discovered or rediscovered; the most esoteric teachings of the East are being searched out by increasing numbers of avid seekers. Western interpreters of the East — Gurdjieff, Ouspensky, Huxley, and more recently, Leary and Alpert — have found a growing new audience. And in addition to the vast core of youths who are regularly practicing formal techniques, there exists an even larger peripheral group of "spiritual seekers." Some have merely begun to read about the East, others have dabbled with macrobiotics, and a surprising number has completely given up city life to farm in remote rural areas, often grouping together into "spiritual communes." Though the members may not practice an actual discipline on a regular basis, their lifestyles often closely approximate that of an Indian *ashram* — a true Eastern religious commune.

In short, American interest in Eastern philosophies has not only risen dramatically in public visibility, but has expanded even more widely on a grassroots level, among individuals and small groups, from Manhattan apartments to distant country farms. It has been a quiet revolution, lacking the fanfare of LSD use or political activism in the sixties. Yet it is no less significant, and it will probably reach a larger numerical scale than either of those movements. It is simply less conspicuous; most Eastern practitioners (though not all) are more anxious to avoid publicity than to court it. In fact, some of the Eastern organizations are secret; one has chapters in many cities, but its name is almost unknown and it can be joined only by invitation. And many of the other disciplines, such as Zen, though not so closed to outsiders, make no attempt to attract new members. Yet youths are going hundreds of miles to seek them out, even leaving their old lives behind to voyage to India or Japan. Despite its quietness, the swell of interest in the East is making itself felt across the continent.

THE EAST AND THE SPIRITUAL SUBCULTURES

But to be more specific: what is meant by "the East?" What is encompassed by the term "Eastern disciplines?" Is it truly a widespread phenomenon? Is it really new? For the purposes of this book, one might arrange the "spiritual" pursuits of American youths along a continuum, from the most scientific to the most mystical. At one end are techniques, not strictly spiritual, which involve technical experimentation with altered states of consciousness, such as alpha wave conditioning. In the same category would also fall scientology, a technique of recent Western invention. Though its actual scientific merits are debated, it clearly carries a scientific ethos, even in its name. Techniques based on Western psychology and psychiatry, such as sensitivity group training, encounter groups, and many of the recently popular forms of avant-garde psychotherapy, would be included in the "scientific" category, as would experimentation with LSD and other hallucinogens. Though LSD use may lead to mystic experiences and states of consciousness far beyond the domain of ordinary science, it remains for the purposes of this classification a scientific method, since it is based on a chemical.

At the other end of the continuum lie the most clearly magical and antiscientific techniques, such as witchcraft and black magic. The various forms of divination, including Tarot cards, the I Ching, and astrology, would also fall close to the magical extreme. Though some claim to be remarkably successful, the magical techniques promise more circumscribed results than other spiritual disciplines. They do not aspire to improve an individual's entire life or to raise his consciousness, but merely to give him specific powers.

Between the scientific and magical extremes, but somewhat closer to the latter, one might place the "theological" disciplines: those based on the worship of a deity. A number of American youth subcultures have formed around theological beliefs. The "Jesus freaks" are the best-known example, but a number of other Western theological systems have found new support as well.

Finally, the lion's share of the continuum, the expanse from the border of science over to the edge of theology, is occupied by the spectrum of Eastern disciplines. At the scientific end are disciplines based on a specific, clearly defined technique, such as Transcendental Meditation. TM, as it is often called, is not a religion at all, and Maharishi Mahesh Yogi, though greatly respected by his followers, is never treated as a divinity. He is merely the teacher of a systematic method of daily meditation. In fact, the underlying philosophy of TM is called the "science of creative intelligence," the word "science" being justified on the grounds that anyone can experimentally prove its claims by practicing TM himself and experiencing the results. Not only that, but TM offers numerous journal articles documenting the physiological effects and psychological benefits of meditation — legitimate laboratory studies, though perhaps not so well controlled as a hard-core scientist would prefer. In general, TM has been quite successful in its appeal to the scientific atmosphere of the West.

Also near the scientific extreme, one finds many other Eastern disciplines based on the daily practice of a specific technique, such as Ananda Marga, Tibetan Buddhism, and the various forms of Yoga. Yoga, in fact, spans quite a broad area, from highly Westernized, purely physical methods for maintaining well-being (the kind practiced even by Wall Street businessmen), to techniques which retain all of their Eastern character and require a much deeper commitment, such as the yoga practiced by the followers of Kirpal Singh.

Traveling away from the scientific end of the continuum, one first passes through techniques which require an entire life-discipline, rather than the practice of a single technique. This would include, for example, the spiritual lifestyle of a Zen commune or that of a Kirpal Singh ashram. Approaching theology, one would next find groups such as the lovers of Guru Maharaj Ji or Meher Baba, who feel that the master, though visibly a human being, is in another sense divine. Finally, crossing the border into theology, one encounters actual Eastern religions as opposed to disciplines, such as the Hare Krishna group. Krishna is an actual god, worshipped by his followers in a temple. They rise in the night or early morning to pray, and are required to observe chastity until married, a feature more suggestive of Western religion than of Eastern techniques. Nicherin Shoshu, as the Manhattan scenario suggests, is also a true religion, though not as rigorous and involving as Krishna.

Two categories of "Eastern techniques" do not fit quite as neatly onto the continuum. The first of these is a group of "martial arts." Like yoga, the martial arts of the East range from techniques which have been totally Westernized for the sole purpose of self-defense (Karate, Judo), to those which retain a predominantly spiritual character (Tai Chi). Tai Chi is clearly a true Eastern discipline, much closer to Yoga than to self-defense. For this reason it should probably be classed with the other Eastern disciplines, although, as it happens, I have not quoted any practitioners of Tai Chi in these pages. The other martial arts, however, seem too far removed from their Eastern origins to put in the same category.

Macrobiotics and related diets are also difficult to classify. Many are of Eastern origin, and in a sense they are disciplines, but I have chosen, somewhat arbitrarily, not to include them within the area covered by this book. Of course a great number of people who eat macrobiotic diets are also practitioners of Eastern techniques; only those who are involved *exclusively* with macrobiotics are not covered by the present classification. However, much of what is said in the following pages, particularly in chapters three and seven, would apply to the macrobiotic group as well.

This, then, is the range of Eastern disciplines: from daily yoga and meditation over to full-scale religions. In the pages that follow, *Eastern disciplines* and *Eastern techniques* will be used synonymously, despite the fact that some of the groups do not in fact practice an actual discipline or technique. The lovers of Meher Baba, for instance, seek only to love Baba; they practice no exercises or daily routines. Unfortunately, there exists no better phrase than "Eastern disciplines" to cover the entire range. Also synonymous in this book are the terms *Eastern practitioners* and *meditators.* Although most of the Eastern disciplines involve at least some form of meditation, several do not; the word "meditators" is used simply for lack of a better single word to describe the entire class of youths on the road East. Throughout this book, in other words, the reader must be wary of the fact that the above terms have been expanded to a wider meaning than usual.

Given these definitions, we can now ask the size of the Eastern subculture in this country. How many Americans are involved in Eastern disciplines? Of all subcultural groups, they are one of the most difficult to count. Many live on remote farms or spiritual communes in the country, in deliberate retreat from the computerized society which likes to count people. Others lead very orthodox lives and hold the most ordinary jobs, but do a set of yoga asanas or Zen meditation every evening in their apartments. Even their friends may not know of their interest in the East. In short, it would seem impossible to offer more than a vague estimate of the size of the Eastern subculture. However, several of the highly organized Eastern schools in this country keep track of their number of followers. Nicherin Shoshu Buddhism, for instance, claims about 100,000 American practitioners, and the followers of Guru Maharaj Ji are reputed to be approaching the 100,000 mark as well. The most accurate records are those of Transcendental Meditation, which listed 232,118 Americans initiated up to mid-June 1973. All of these figures are rising almost exponentially. The TM group, for example, has been doubling every two years, and so far shows no signs of levelling off; initiations in fall 1973 were numbering 20,000 a month. The doubling time for the Guru Maharaj Ji group is currently even shorter.

Despite these figures, it is still difficult to estimate the size of the total Eastern group. A minor problem is that some youths may be counted twice, such as those who began doing Transcendental Meditation and then converted over to Guru Maharaj Ji when he became well known in 1972. The major problem is that Zen and the many forms of Yoga — which include far more practitioners than the previous groups, possess no nationwide organization and are thus uncountable. And in addition to this, there are dozens — perhaps over a hundred — less well known disciplines spread all over the country, each with its modest but growing group of followers.

Nevertheless, there exists one elegantly simple way to assess the size of the entire Eastern subculture. This is to take a random population, count the number who have been involved in one or another of the Eastern disciplines, then count the subset of that group who have at some point been initiated into Transcendental Meditation. Given the ratio of "TM" respondents to the entire group of "Eastern" respondents, and knowing the number of Transcendental Meditators initiated nationwide up to that time, one can extrapolate to the size of the Eastern subculture as a whole. For instance, the equation for June 1973 would be:

$$\text{Total number of Eastern practitioners in the U.S.A.} = \frac{\text{Number of respondents who have practiced any Eastern disciplines}}{\text{Number of respondents who have been initiated into TM}} \times 232{,}118$$

Of course this yields the number of people who have practiced an Eastern discipline at some time; one can correct it, if desired, for the number practicing an Eastern discipline at the current time. Notice that the results will be accurate *regardless* of what proportion of Eastern practitioners one finds in the population sampled: whether 1 percent or 90 percent of the respondents have practiced an Eastern discipline is irrelevant to the determination. The only major possibility for error would be if the population were likely to contain, say, a disproportionate number of Zen meditators relative to Transcendental Meditators, or too few yoga practitioners relative to Transcendental Meditators. All that is required, in other words, is that the population represent Transcendental Meditators fairly in comparison to the other groups. We seek only a proportion, not an absolute number, and thus the only error will be, in effect, second-order error.

With this in mind, I left a large pile of appropriate questionnaires at Erewhon Trading Post, Boston's best-known organic food store. Erewhon was very helpful, as always; when I returned a week later, two boxes had appeared, one marked "mystical questionnaires" and one marked "fulfilled questionnaires." Of the completed questionnaires that accumulated in the "fulfilled" box, 86 were from people who had at some time practiced an Eastern discipline. Of these, 78, or more than 90 percent, replied that they were practicing some Eastern discipline at the current time, and the majority of those stated that they practiced quite regularly. Of the group of 86, a total of 19 replied that they had been initiated into Transcendental Meditation. Of these, only 9, or less than 50 percent, were still practicing TM, and most of the remaining 10 had moved into other Eastern techniques.

The study was performed in late July 1973. The total number of Transcendental Meditators initiated up to that time in the United States was 245,000, plus or minus 3,000 (this total is obtained by taking the 232,000 figure for June and adding an approximate 13,000 initiates for the period from June to July). Thus the estimate for total Eastern practitioners is 86/19 x 245,000, or slightly more than 1.1 million. The number currently practicing an Eastern technique would then be just over one million.

One million people. This is an impressive number, but it is probably too conservative, because the Erewhon sample is likely to contain a *larger* proportion of Transcendental Meditators than the Eastern subculture as a whole. First, Transcendental Meditation is numerically much stronger in Boston than it is in many comparable cities. As a result, it is probably more heavily represented in this sample than are other disciplines which are less skewed toward Boston as opposed to other areas. Secondly, since Transcendental Meditation demands less of a change of lifestyle than many techniques, its followers are somewhat less likely to inhabit remote farms or rural ashrams. Therefore, sampling in an urban area may again slightly favor Transcendental Meditation over other techniques. Third, Transcendental Meditators are more likely to buy organic food than practitioners of many other disciplines. For example, Nicherin Shoshu Buddhism, despite its American following of 100,000, was not represented by a single individual among the 86 respondents. The reason is that there is little emphasis on organic food in Nicherin Shoshu, but a good deal in TM. Thus we have several reasons to believe that Transcendental Meditators are overrepresented at Erewhon, and that the calculated estimate for total Eastern practitioners is therefore too low. One million people, then, is a bare minimum. The actual figure may exceed one and a half million, and it is rapidly growing.

The questionnaires were remarkable for the diversity of disciplines that they included. Many respondents listed two or three different techniques that they had tried, and some even stated that they were practicing several techniques at the same time. About 40 respondents listed some form of yoga; a number wrote just the word "yoga," but many were more specific: Hatha Yoga, Kundalini Yoga, Kriya Yoga, Integral Yoga, Bhakti Yoga, Raja Yoga, Tantric Yoga, and others. More than 20 respondents mentioned Zen. Five respondents were followers of Guru Maharaj Ji, and the names of several other masters appeared: Kirpal Singh, Ramana Maharshi, Ramakrishna, and Chogyam Trungpa. Also represented were Ananda Marga, Tibetan Buddhism, Hare Krishna, Sufism, Taoist Meditation, and Tai Chi. Of the large Eastern groups, only Meher Baba and Nicherin Shoshu did not appear.

The age distribution of the respondents was also interesting: more than 90 percent of the 86 respondents were between eighteen and thirty, and nearly 70 percent were in the even narrower band between twenty and twenty-six. This agrees well with my experience from participant observation; the great majority of the meditators that I have met were in that age group. The word "youths" in the remainder of this book refers to the age span from eighteen to thirty, although much of what is said would apply to the other 10 percent of younger or older meditators as well. In ordinary English usage, "youth" is rarely considered to extend to age thirty, but I have used it, partially for lack of a better single word to describe the entire age range from eighteen to thirty, and partially because youth, as a period of life, is extending to an older chronological age in modern times and in our culture.

Of course a few meditators are much older; in every group one meets an occasional man or woman in the fifties or sixties. But often, despite their age, the older people became involved in Eastern disciplines for much the same reasons as their younger counterparts. The oldest member of the Erewhon sample was 62, aside from one respondent who stated that his age was 307. The latter claimed to have been practicing Eastern techniques for 305 years, "ever since the birth of my consciousness." On the question of whether he was currently practicing a technique, he replied, "No, I became very disillusioned with them — too many amateurs." Not a surprising attitude, perhaps: one might easily tire of all the novices after the first few centuries. The same respondent also stated that he had been initiated into Transcendental Meditation, but unfortunately I was forced to discard his questionnaire for computational purposes, since he failed to specify whether he had been initiated during his present incarnation or a previous one.

The 300-year-old respondent brings to mind the last question: are Eastern disciplines really a recent development in this country? Is the whole thing really new? Of course it is not entirely new; there has been a trickle of Eastern philosophy into our hemisphere for at least a century, and "spiritual" youth subcultures, both here and abroad, have occurred frequently throughout history. The "back to nature" movement of German youth prior to World War II, to mention only one example, has much in common with the philosophy of meditators today. But interest in the East, specifically, has never reached a scale in America comparable to that which we see today: never has there been such a proliferation of techniques taught around the country, such a multitude of highly organized groups with computerized address lists, national newspapers, and extensive campaigns to attract new members. Not only in organic food stores or on university campuses, but in office buildings, barber shops, supermarkets, big-city newspapers, bumper stickers, even on television, one sees pictures of Maharishi Mahesh Yogi, Guru Maharaj Ji, and other popular Eastern teachers. Well-known public figures are practicing Transcendental Meditation and expounding its virtues; newspaper articles about it have even reached the *Wall Street Journal.* Guru Maharaj Ji is currently filling 15,000-person auditoriums across the nation, and he will probably succeed in filling the Astrodome in November. In a numerical sense, at least, the current Eastern movement has far outstripped any previous episode in American history. Having easily passed the million mark, it shows every sign of growing further.

But size is not the only novel feature of the modern Eastern subculture. It also represents a massive new opposition to technology and science, even a rejection of the philosophical foundations of Western thought. Our national history has included an occasional Thoreau, a few utopian communities, but in general Americans have hardly been characterized by opposition to technological development. Now, rather abruptly, a vast contingent of youth, including a striking proportion of the most sophisticated and highly educated, has all but abandoned it. Indeed, if the reader has not mingled with meditators or heard them speak, he may be quite unprepared for some of the quotations that we will hear in succeeding chapters. The reaction to science goes surprisingly deep; hundreds of thousands of youths have discarded it both in their lives and in their thought.

What triggered their exodus? What brought them to the road East? The answer begins with another novel development of recent times: the hallucinogenic drug scene.

A SOLUTION TO THE DRUG PROBLEM

How curiously appropriate, the Eastern master Hari Dass Baba has suggested, that to enlighten the most materialistic country in the world, God sent, not his son, but a material: a drug called LSD. For beyond a doubt, the advent of LSD, and the subsequent growth of a drug sub-culture around it, were the key events that directly or indirectly started a million American youths on the road East.

How did it happen? Authorities had preached that drug "abuse" was anything but a step on the path to enlightenment; it was a dead end, an evil that could hardly create valuable results on the far side. Especially during the late sixties, many adults saw the drug scene as a tera-toid growth, spreading relentlessly across the country, swallowing up increasing numbers of innocent youths who would never emerge. But that did not occur. Instead of spreading freely, the drug epidemic rapidly reached a plateau and stopped. Possibly it is even receding, although this is quite likely a result of decreased publicity, since the modal age for drug use has shifted away from the college years and down to the high-school level. And drug use in local high schools, however widespread, is certainly a less sensational topic for the national media than was LSD when it made its debut at Berkeley and Harvard. At any rate, the size of drug culture has approached a state of equilibrium: youths are entering it and exiting from it at approximately equal rates. A modest degree of involvement in drug use has

21

become, in the opinion of many observers, a "normal" stage of adolescent development, rather like adolescent sexual experimentation: a
stage entered typically near the beginning of high school and lasting
from a few months to a few years. A very large fraction of the youths
now starting college have already done a stint of heavy marijuana
smoking, tried LSD or other major hallucinogens a few times, perhaps
even dabbled with cocaine or heroin, then left it all behind. Now they
are only recreational users of marijuana, a practice which in many parts
of this country is approaching the social acceptability of alcohol use.

What has blunted the drug subculture? What truncated its growth?
Was it Operation Intercept, more police on the beat, or tougher legal
sanctions? Anyone having even a marginal familiarity with the drug
culture would have to agree that these have been abysmally unsuccess-
ful. During Operation Intercept, for instance, the price of marijuana
rose only transiently and insignificantly; at the worst, the cost of getting stoned was still only a fourth as great as for getting decently drunk.
Excluding the case of heroin detection, all but the most rabid officials
have had to concede that the proportion of drugs seized is minute, the
number of prosecutions small, and the ratio of convictions to total
drug "abusers," statistically negligible. Not only that, but most users,
and even drug dealers, regard the illegality affectionately, treat it with
a certain relish; without the cops, the thrill would be gone. The law,
in short, has hardly dented the drug culture and perhaps, paradoxically,
even encouraged it.

Is it education, then, that has attenuated drug use? Are youths now
better informed as to the dangers? The answer to both questions is
yes. Not only have youths learned what kinds of drug use are dangerous, but equally important, they have learned what kinds are not.
Many parents, inevitably, lag behind the sophistication of their children, still blindly lumping all forms of drug use into a single evil
category. But a substantial part of the older generation has come to
classify marijuana use, and even a touch of harder drug experimentation, on a par with the other impenetrable and slightly risky activities
to which their teen-agers are prone. Warm thanks are due to the vast
number of individuals and groups, both public and private, who joined
in the educational effort. They not only enlightened the two generations, but in many very moving instances, opened communications
between them for the first time. One must exclude from such con-

sideration a certain number of individuals, including a regrettable number of supposed "authorities," who deliberately exaggerated or misrepresented the dangers. For when users discovered that such propaganda was false, as most did, it not only reinforced their distrust of the Establishment, but deafened them to other, more sincere voices. And then, navigating totally on their own, some encountered real dangers. As a result, the propagandists indirectly stimulated what they were striving to suppress. But the overall effect of education has been good; young drug users to whom I talk today can assess the medical and psychiatric liabilities of drugs much more accurately than their counterparts five years ago.

But the bulk of the learning was not didactic; it was achieved by the users on their own. Some learned it the hard way, through hair-raising experiences (a number of which we shall hear recounted in future chapters), but practically all emerged unscathed. Many parents — the names of a few come at once to mind — would be astonished to learn of the brushes with crime, poisoning, and the law that their own children have silently undergone, and all the more astonishing, that those apparently naïve children could recuperate, even profit, from so many near-disasters. One hears of course of the 1 percent who did not make it; the boy with a household-word family name found murdered on the Lower East Side, the rock singer who allegedly died of an overdose, the charming local girl rumored to be in a mental institution after taking LSD. But the vast majority of youths, though some weathered incredible insults, are perfectly intact, to the amazed relief of many older people who had perhaps forgotten to take into account the physiological and psychological resilience of younger minds and bodies.

Not only did they emerge unharmed, but they emerged wiser, with respect for themselves, greater self-knowledge, a more accurate vision of both their powers and limits, and in some, even a newfound reverence for the simple joys of being alive. Also from the drug subculture many acquired clusters of deeply embedded fears and anxieties, tenacious beliefs which have persisted long after the last experience with hallucinogens, amphetamines, or sedatives. But all in all, despite psychiatric pronouncements about the regressive nature of drug use, most youths emerged with a definite, often hard-won, increment of maturity.

The drug subculture has reached equilibrium at a level determined not so much by the intervention of the outside society as by forces within itself. Youths have entered the drug scene, passed some time in it, and then either as a result of satiation or of unpleasant experiences, moved out of it again.

But then, this is not quite true. For in another sense, the Establishment very firmly arrested the growth of the drug culture. Spontaneously, and quite unconsciously, the Establishment did something that nobody seemed to have clearly predicted, yet which, in retrospect, we all should have known it would do. Its technique was insidious, yet vastly more potent, more effectively stifling, than any combination of legal sanctions or police controls: quite simply, like an amoeba, it absorbed the drug culture and digested it.

How did it succeed? First, by making drug use respectable. Ten years ago, even five years ago in some quarters, marijuana was a clandestine, in-group experience among middle- to upper-class youth, shared only by the few. The need for secrecy, the threat of the law, and common acquaintance with a drug that still horrified the outside world, bound users into a select fraternity, a special group with an *esprit de corps* that was even more rewarding than the thrill of the drug experiences themselves. And if marijuana was special, certainly the big hallucinogens — LSD, mescaline, psilocybin, DMT — were truly the forbidden fruit. But then, a rapidly increasing number of unbearably respectable people not only became familiar with marijuana, not only began to pardon it, but worse, tried it themselves. Marijuana diffused out to psychiatrists and college professors, invaded businessmen's gatherings and cocktail parties, and ultimately, permeated suburbia. Even LSD was tried by a number of extremely straight people; it no longer seems entirely implausible when one sees the classic cartoon of two vested, cigar-smoking businessmen where one is saying, "What if I told you that I doubled my profits for fiscal '72 after taking a trip?"

Of course, the social respectability of marijuana or other drugs is hardly universal; the interior of the continent, in particular, is not so free-thinking as the coasts. And the law, characteristically, lags behind the tenor of the times. The penalties for marijuana use are in some areas still monstrous; occasionally one still hears anachronistic pleas for their enforcement. But in general, marijuana, once the foundation of the drug subculture, the mainstay of its *esprit de corps*, has become hopelessly, irrevocably, bourgeois.

A second digestive force of the Establishment, requiring little comment, was commercialization. At first it was harmless: a few head shops selling smoking accessories, some unexpected trends in clothing sales, a handful of record companies capitalizing on the success of acid rock. But soon the drug culture found itself identified and evaluated as a class of consumers, its tastes broadcast throughout the nation, its current interests instantly converted to cheap fads, its appeal systematically exploited for the mass market. Long hair materialized in magazine and television advertisements, psychedelic billboards sprouted on the highways, and "hippie" clothing, at prices real hippies would never pay, appeared on the mannequins in store windows and on adults in the streets. Instinctively realizing that commercialization was dissolving their cultural integrity, drug users reacted with a mixture of dismay and resentment. I recall, in this connection, a spring riot three years ago in Harvard Square: the very first window to be smashed belonged to a posh clothing store — specializing exclusively in "hippie" fashions — which had lamely pretended in its advertisements to be *au courant* with the drug scene.

Third, the Establishment digested the drug subculture by saturation coverage. No sooner had drug use become visible than the nation responded with a massive outpouring of newspaper and magazine articles, television documentaries, movies, books, pamphlets, and programs. The search for news invaded the remotest recesses of the drug scene, ferreted out its every idiosyncrasy for public display. It was endlessly condemned and romanticized — especially the latter — to appease the national appetite. And when that appetite was finally satisfied, when the last drops of juicy copy had been wrung from it, its dessicated remains fell into the jaws of a thousand agencies, officials, educational programs, and task forces which had sprung up in the interim. And again it suffered a loss of cultural integrity, of specialness. It was transformed from a private fraternity to a public affair, from an esoteric cult to a platitude.

Fourth, the drug culture was infiltrated by another characteristic element of American society: crime. Dealing — once the domain of gentle "heads" and upper class college students — quickly became big business and thus a far more dangerous affair. Though organized crime still tends to prefer heroin, it has joined petty thieves, muggers, rip-off artists, and other representatives of the underworld in the lesser forms of drug dealing. Crime has eroded the drug subculture from inside by making the street scene increasingly unpalatable, raising the risks of dealing, and driving the more timid fraction of potential drug users away from the scene entirely.

Fifth, partially as a result of the foregoing changes, a shift has occurred in the species of drugs used. LSD, the drug of the old-time flower children, has declined, and with it a certain carefree, child-like atmosphere that once pervaded the subculture. Now the atmosphere is older, less spontaneous, less experimental, and drug use has moved toward alcohol, sedatives, and tranquilizers. Having once scorned the tranquilizer abuse of the older generation — witness the Rolling Stones' famous song "Mother's Little Helper," in which the "helper" is a "little yellow pill" — youths now have to confess that they are abusing the yellow pills themselves. With suburbia now turning on and its children popping tranquilizers, the drug use of the two generations is converging asymptotically.

In short, though the drug subculture is little changed in size, its *raison d'etre* is vanishing. The old thrills are gone, the risks are up, and the whole thing has become too damned respectable, anyway. The Establishment, in a word, has found the solution to the drug problem: a solution by dissolution, as it were. Or more accurately, by disillusion: it has deprived the subculture of its principal forms of appeal. For not only is the fun decreased, but drug use no longer answers many of the other needs of youths. It has ceased to be an effective way to withdraw from society, and it fails to adequately express anger at parents or authority figures. It lacks the philosophical and psychological justifications that it once had. Most of all, it has lost the single most rewarding feature of the deviant subculture: the ability to give its members a sense of belonging, of identity. Its once-sharp boundaries have dissolved to a blur; it has been homogenized into the larger culture. Youths have thus been denied the satisfaction of defining themselves as insiders as opposed to outsiders; the distinction is gone. Having lost an identity, where to turn? It was at this point that several hundred thousand drug users looked to the East.

·   ·   ·

Of course not all drug users took up Eastern disciplines. A few went on to other pleasure-seeking groups such as the swinging scene or the homosexual subculture. Another small segment from the activist extreme of the drug world became immersed in political activities or women's liberation. A somewhat larger number continued to use drugs heavily, but most of them discarded hallucinogens in favor of alcohol, barbiturates, opiates, and other sedatives. A still larger group became interested in macrobiotics and organic farming, and retreated to the country to homestead on their own. This group of course overlaps with the Eastern group; about half of the members of the "organic" culture have tried an Eastern discipline for at least some period of time. Other small groups of former drug users became "Jesus freaks," experimented with other altered states of consciousness, or became interested in magic. And a substantial fraction of the members of the drug world did not transfer to a new youth subculture at all, but simply returned to college, started jobs, or otherwise resumed a more orthodox American lifestyle. Of course, it is difficult to quantify the size of all of these various migrations out of the drug subculture. But almost certainly, Eastern disciplines absorbed the largest single group of former drug users. In a decade, even half a decade, a whole range of Eastern disciplines rose from insignificant groups to organizations with thousands and even hundreds of thousands of followers. And the bulk of that population came from the drug world.

This is not to say that interest in the East was entirely created by the efflux from the drug subculture. Of course, Eastern disciplines had existed on a small scale in the United States before. Meher Baba was known in this country a generation ago; in 1936 Paramahansa Yogananda had founded the Self-Realization Fellowship Hermitage in California to teach Kriya Yoga; Alan Watts had begun writing about Zen in the late fifties. But the number of actual practitioners of Eastern techniques then was minute in comparison to today. It must also be acknowledged that the recent surge of interest is not exclusively due to the drug subculture. A certain number of youths have become involved in Eastern disciplines without having previously flirted with drugs. But even the interest of many of these youths was, in a sense, indirectly sparked by the drug scene, because without former drug users to swell its ranks, Eastern philosophy in America would not have become so prominent or well known that it could come to the attention of many outsiders. Furthermore, many drug users, having begun to practice an Eastern discipline themselves, persuaded non-drug-using friends, younger siblings, and even their parents to join.

In 1972, to test the above impressions, I performed a brief quantitative study on the former drug use of Transcendental Meditators. Of 59 randomly chosen meditators in Cambridge, Massachusetts, 86 percent reported that they had used marijuana, and 54 percent reported that they had used LSD or another hallucinogen at some time. If one discounts the small fraction of meditators over thirty years of age (about 10 percent), the drug figures are even higher: over 90 percent for marijuana, over 60 percent for LSD, and over 40 percent for amphetamines. Probably the drug figures would not be quite so high for 59 meditators in, say, Kansas, but then there are vastly more meditators on the coasts than in the midwest. One cannot be certain that comparable figures would apply to other Eastern disciplines, but it is my impression from participant observation that they would: in fact some of the Eastern groups appear to draw an even larger fraction of their members from the drug subculture than does Transcendental Meditation. In short, there is little doubt that the drug subculture played an overwhelming role in the rise of the East; drug users, plus the friends and relatives they later attracted, probably account for more than 90 percent of the million practitioners of Eastern disciplines. As a result, this book seeks primarily to explain the evolution of those youths: from the drug scene to the road East.

A NEW SUBCULTURE

Why did so many youths choose to go East? What does the East offer over other subcultures? First, unlike the drug culture, it is indigestible, less easily molested by the Establishment. For instance, it is refreshingly immune to commercialization. The most canny corporation can hardly clear a profit from meditation communes or yoga students. And though a cute long-haired hippie couple, promoting cosmetics or clothes or automobiles in a psychedelic-colored magazine ad, can drain a certain amount from public pocketbooks, it is a bit difficult to imagine Guru Maharaj Ji endorsing toothpaste or Zen masters plugging diet cola. Nor is the East so vulnerable to the media. It is not sensational enough, not juicy enough to merit saturation coverage. And, in comparison to drugs, it is inscrutable. The drug culture spawned "authorities" on the subject *ad nauseum*, but few claim expertise in the wisdom of the East; the real authorities are inscrutable themselves. Finally — to invoke a word foreign to the media — the Eastern disciplines are sacred. However new they may be in this country, most techniques have centuries of religious tradition behind them. And though some commentators dismiss the East as another trivial fad, it is harder to denigrate it, to cheapen it, than in the case of the hippies.

As a result, Eastern disciplines represent a more successful way for a youth to withdraw from the Establishment and remain permanently out of reach of its tentacles. Not only does it serve as a physical or emotional withdrawal, as drugs once did very well, but beyond that, it represents for many youths a much more profound intellectual withdrawal: a wholesale rejection of modern medicine and technology, of the scientific methods, of Aristotelian logic, and of Western definitions of validity, credibility, and even sanity. The immensity of this rejection must be witnessed to be appreciated; when one has been brought up thinking that $A = B$ and $B = C$ implies $A = C$, it can be unnerving to converse with a group of people who, in effect, don't believe in it. We shall listen to a few such conversations later.

Secondly, the East is safer than drugs. In particular, it offers welcome relief to youths who suffered frightening experiences during their involvement with the drug subculture: overdoses, bad health, encounters with criminals or law officials, some of which will be recounted in the next two chapters. The Eastern subculture offers what the drug scene once offered but now has lost: gentleness and love. In fact, many of the old-time hippies of the mid-sixties, the ones who threw flowers at the police and staged love-ins in the park, are among the most dedicated and influential members of the Eastern subculture today. And not only has the East inherited the gentleness of the flower children, but it promises a less tangible kind of safety, a safety which the drug culture could never adequately supply: relief from anxiety. And anxiety, as we shall hear later, can reach terrible levels in the lives of many American youths.

Drug use was once also a way to express anger at parents or society. Some anger was expressed directly, in the sense that drug users did things that were either socially disapproved or downright illegal, while

broadcasting an anti-Establishment philosophy. But as I have suggested previously (*Voices from the Drug Culture* pp. 43-47), a greater
portion of the anger was released in indirect, manipulative ways: by
baiting the fantasies of the older generation (which, predictably, dis-
guised its envy with rage) or by means of self-destructive behavior.
One might think the East a poor substitute for the drug culture as a
way to express anger, but in fact Eastern disciplines can easily be
molded to fit the purpose, particularly if they are misinterpreted a
bit. Chapter six will illustrate some covert ways in which anger and
aggression are successfully expressed by a certain fraction of Eastern
practitioners.

Not only does the East offer emotional satisfactions analogous to
those of the drug culture at its best, but the techniques, in the minds
of many drug users, act as a direct substitute for the drug experiences
themselves. Many youths, quite simply, were seeking a new way to get
high, preferably a more permanent way, and one that lacked the increasing liabilities of the drug scene. On a more intellectual level numerous writers, such as Aldous Huxley and later Leary and Alpert, had already drawn the parallel between hallucinogenic experiences and Eastern mystical ones. LSD, as Hari Dass Baba predicted, whetted but did
not satisfy the appetites of thousands of users, particularly the more
sophisticated and well-educated ones. With hallucinogens they glimpsed
an entire new plane of mental experience, felt unity with the cosmos,
weathered the death-rebirth trip. And then, instinctively realizing
that there was something incredibly fundamental about those experiences and that state of consciousness, something which transcended the
divisions of history and culture, and ignoring ridiculous quibbles about
whether the thing had been a "valid" religious experience or not, they
looked to the East as the logical way to continue their search and perhaps more permanently grasp that elusive understanding. This small
group of youths — I call them, in chapter eight, the "sphere-searchers"
— has formed much of the intellectual elite of Eastern disciplines in
America, the vanguard of seekers who in turn drew a much larger number of other drug users behind them. Often they are the ones who experimented most heavily with LSD, read most avidly about mysticism
and altered states of consciousness, then abruptly stopped, converted
completely to an Eastern technique, and went on to attract new followers with missionary devotion.

Finally, there are a few who have reached the East directly, on the basis of their own experiences and knowledge, without any prior drug experiences or even any contact with drug users. Some of these are much older people, but a few are youths who through reading, conversations, or contact with the right people, reasoned that there must be something genuine in the wisdom of the East and recognized that they could only learn of it by experiencing it themselves. Many of this group might also fall into the "intellectual elite" category. But the entire group is small in numbers; as stated before, the vast majority of young meditators either used drugs themselves or were directly influenced by drug users.

Up to this point we have outlined primarily the psychological appeal of the East, the ways in which it replaces the drug culture as a means to satisfy personal desires of youths. But it is also a social phenomenon, the substitution of a new youth subculture for the old. As a sharply demarcated subculture, one that has not been dissolved into the larger society, the Eastern subculture offers the same social benefits that the drug subculture once offered in its former, more intact state. Most simply, Eastern disciplines bring youths together as friends, friends who share not only the technique they practice, but a whole cluster of values as well: opposition to technocracy, emphasis on the spiritual as opposed to the material, and gentleness as opposed to aggressiveness. New practitioners enter a supportive, warm environment, filled with enthusiastic peers, and relatively free of aggression and competition. Both as students of a particular discipline and as members of the larger group of youths on the road East, they derive a sense of specialness, a feeling that they are linked to a great throng of other spiritual seekers. Though they have left the drug world behind, they have recaptured one of its greatest gifts: the subcultural *esprit de corps.*

With it they have regained something even more precious: a sense of identity. Not only are they again amidst allies, but they feel that they are doing something significant, that they have an important activity around which to define themselves and their lives. Years ago, heavy LSD use once served the same purpose; many acid-heads, taking hallucinogens three times a week, justified their use on a similar basis. They defined it as a philosophical or psychological quest, not "kicks" but serious business, a life-task of central importance. And in the empathetic, insulated core of the drug subculture, they were supported in their commitment; the LSD quest was an accepted foundation on which to build a satisfying sense of identity. A few acid-heads still attempt to use LSD in this way, but in the modern, disintegrated drug scene, it is much harder to convince others, or themselves, that their identity is legitimate. Now, however, the spiritual quest of Eastern disciplines offers a similar, but far more solid basis for identity than LSD in its prime. Admittedly, a portion of the public ridicules the East as well, but in general, Eastern techniques are infinitely more respectable than hallucinogens.

The identity-value of the Eastern subculture is particularly evident in some youths when they seek to defend their disciplines to skeptical outsiders. Some will dogmatically maintain that theirs is the One True Path to enlightenment, and many, while allowing that different techniques would probably work, argue that their technique is more efficient, produces more rapid evolution, than any of the others. For example, I recall a conversation that I had with another practitioner of Transcendental Meditation, named Ray.

"What do you think about the other Eastern methods? Do you think they work?" I asked.

He laughed. "Most of them are just mood-making. They're just ways to put yourself into some pleasant state where you think you're advancing, but actually you're just entertaining yourself."

"What about Zen? Don't you think that works?"

"Well, the problem with Zen is that it involves concentration. You have to fixate your mind on something when you meditate. I know because I've talked to a couple of people who do Zen. And if you're concentrating on something, that's the worst thing you can do. It just makes it all the harder for your mind to break away and get down to the source of thought the way you do in TM. So if you get to cosmic consciousness in Zen you'd have to do it in spite of Zen, if you see what I mean."

"Well, how about Ananda Marga? They use a technique that's very close to TM."

"It's similar, I know, but it involves both concentration *and* contemplation. So it holds you back the same way Zen does, keeps your mind from getting away from thought and

down to the absolute." He laughed again. "I know a couple
of guys from TM who went off and tried Ananda Marga for
awhile. But they both came back. People always come back
to TM."

"Well, do you think that there are people who can get to
cosmic consciousness by other routes? Or maybe be born
with it? What about somebody like Guru Maharaj Ji?"

"Oh, you mean that fifteen-year-old kid? I've never actually seen him, but I've talked to some people who are into
that scene, and they're sort of screwed-up people. They
certainly didn't look to me like they were going anywhere.
And anyhow, Guru what's-his-face is just a kid. He's got
pinball machines and electric trains, and all that kind of
thing!"

"Can't you play pinball when you're in cosmic consciousness?"

"Well — you know what I mean."

"But what about my previous question? Do you think
that people can get to cosmic consciousness by other
routes, like someone who leads a regular life in the West,
for instance?"

"In the West? That's pretty tough if you don't have
TM. The West is so fucked up that you'd have to be
pretty incredible to end up in CC all by yourself in the
West. That's obvious!"

Of course not all practitioners of Transcendental Meditation are so
intolerant of other disciplines as Ray. Nor, conversely, is the intolerance unique to Transcendental Meditators; I have encountered it within every Eastern group that I have visited, among both novices and
experienced teachers. Sometimes it becomes outright fanaticism,
though at the same time one cannot help recalling that the East, through
the centuries, has been a feeble match for the West so far as religious
intolerance is concerned. At any rate, well-reasoned defenses such as
Ray's, his almost catechismic denouncements of alternate paths to enlightenment, suggest a need for certainty, a need to prove that his
activity is correct, legitimate, a sound basis on which to build his
philosophy and self-image. Perhaps, it might be reasoned, there exists
a paucity of solid bases for individual identity in our increasingly ho-

mogeneous and depersonalized culture. Having found an identity in
the Eastern subculture, one that hopefully will be less easily digested,
it is perhaps not unreasonable that Ray defends his technique so vigor-
ously, even to the extent of sharply distinguishing it from its closest
relative.

The value of the subcultural element of Eastern disciplines is difficult to underestimate; in subsequent chapters, we shall repeatedly hear
it demonstrated by other meditators, like Ray, who make a point of
demarcating their disciplines from the rest of the world. For not only
is the subculture a source of friends and a foundation of identity, but
it buffers its members against both concrete fears and vague anxieties,
against guilt, and against both the physical and intellectual influences
of technology.

A CURE FOR DRUG USE?

Before going on to describe further effects of the subculture, one
remaining question deserves reply: do the Eastern techniques actually
"work" to reduce drug use? As the reader may well be aware, several
of the Eastern disciplines, particularly Transcendental Meditation, advertise that they are very effective in doing this. Even high government officials have stood up to take notice: does the East offer new
hope in cases where all previous programs have been ineffective?

The following analysis begins specifically with Transcendental Meditation, though as we shall see, it probably applies to the other techniques as well. Transcendental Meditation, in a resolution adopted by
the House of Representatives of the State of Illinois (Number 677), is
described as showing "promise of being the most positive and effective
drug prevention program being presented in the world today." The
evidence for this rather strong statement is, initially at least, very impressive. A typical study, probably the best-known one (Benson and
Wallace, 1970), involved 1,950 meditators at two meditation training
courses in the summer of 1970. A total of 1,862 of the meditators
returned the questionnaire. Of these, 78 percent stated that they had
used marijuana or hashish during the six months prior to starting meditation. After practicing Transcendental Meditation for six months,
only 37 percent used marijuana, and of those who had meditated more

than twenty-one months, only 12 percent still used marijuana. The figures for LSD were even more impressive. About 48 percent of subjects had used LSD prior to beginning meditation, and this decreased to 12.5 percent after starting meditation. After twenty-one months of meditation, the LSD figure was only 3 percent.

Unfortunately, certain doubts arise as one reads this study. First, was it a random sample of meditators? The questionnaire was distributed to meditators who had paid about $300, and traveled hundreds or thousands of miles, to attend either of two month-long intensive courses in Transcendental Meditation. They were, in other words, the cream of the cream, the most dedicated, committed group of meditators in the country. Therefore they were people who experienced tremendous pressures from within their group, not only to stop using drugs, but to alter their lifestyles completely in favor of Transcendental Meditation. Would the drug results be so impressive with a merely "average" group of meditators? But even an average group would be far from random, for it would fail to include the substantial fraction of youths who were taught the technique and then discontinued it. Surely a legitimate study of the value of Transcendental Meditation would have to sample all who started the technique, *including* those who obtained poor results from it, found it ineffective, or otherwise became disenchanted. It is difficult to assess the size of the disenchanted group, the attrition rate from Transcendental Meditation. Informed sources have told me that it was as high as 60 percent or as low as 15 percent. On the basis of participant-observation, I would place it at about one-third, which is probably lower than the attrition figures for many other Eastern techniques. Given this, it is clearly impossible to extrapolate from data on the most select meditators to the effects of Transcendental Meditation as a whole.

Secondly, even allowing that a decline in drug use could nevertheless be demonstrated in the more general case, one still cannot distinguish between correlation or causality. Were the decisions to start meditation and reduce drug use sequential or merely simultaneous? The decreasing drug use after longer periods of meditation, shown in the study, suggests causality, but numerous plausible alternatives come to mind; for example there may be some common underlying cause, such as fear of poison or of bad health which induces *both* longer commitment to meditation and lower drug use. In addition, as suggested earlier in this chapter, there is good reason to believe that many youths *first* became disillusioned with the drug culture and *then* took up meditation. Once they had become disillusioned, their drug use tapered naturally over the next year or two. The fact that they were meditating may have been purely incidental to the decline. In short, decline in drug use may lead to meditation rather than meditation leading to decline in drug use. If causality exists, in other words, it could well be in precisely the opposite direction to that proposed in the study.

Finally, even conceding that the study might be correct in spite of both the giant problems of randomness and causality, what is there to show that Transcendental Meditation is better than any other Eastern technique, or, for that matter, any other Western youth subculture, in reducing drug use? Is it uniquely the "most positive and effective drug-prevention program" in the world? Unfortunately there exists little comparative data.

As an attempt to answer this and the preceding questions, I performed the small study mentioned earlier in this chapter. The sample of 59 meditators was less highly select than that of Wallace and Benson, though still far from random in that it did not include subjects who had begun meditation and then stopped. However, the results are strikingly similar to theirs: marijuana declined from 86 percent to 42 percent, whereas LSD and other hallucinogens went from 54 percent to 12 percent. Even "average" meditators, then, seem to show a comparable decline in drug use.

However, I then distributed 41 essentially identical questionnaires to customers in Boston's best-known organic food store. One of the respondents was a Transcendental Meditator; 16 more named other techniques (the replies included several forms of yoga, Zen, and a couple of more exotic techniques), and 24 stated that they practiced no Eastern disciplines. Among the 16 "other techniques" subjects, former marijuana use was 94 percent as opposed to present use of only 31 percent, and LSD and other hallucinogens dropped from 69 percent to 6 percent – both declines greater than for the Transcendental Meditators in either my sample or that of Benson and Wallace. The 24 "non-Eastern" subjects went from 92 percent to 46 percent on marijuana, and LSD declined from an astonishing 83 percent to only 12 percent, again greater declines than for the meditators.

Finally, I distributed a third set of questionnaires to a control group:

the customers in an electronics store. Though their age distribution was similar to the two previous groups, their former drug use was not as high as the others. Furthermore, although they exhibited some decline in drug use from past to present, it was significantly smaller than for either the meditators or the organic food customers.

In conclusion, we can begin by presuming that the most spectacular decline in drug use — that of the organic food customers — is not directly *caused* by a mere interest in organic food, but instead correlated with it. Secondly, the decline is not unique to Transcendental Meditation, nor even to Eastern disciplines as a whole; this is also apparent from the organic food group. On the other hand, it is not a universal decline, reflecting simply a national decrease in drug use, for it is nearly absent among the electronics buyers. The common denominator of reduced drug use, then, appears to be the shift in subcultures that the first two groups have both undertaken. For one reason or another, they became dissatisfied with the drug subculture and its chemical philosophy, then moved to a new subculture — Eastern, organic, or both — with philosophical and peer-group pressures of the opposite kind. In short, their lower drug use seems to be only the natural concomitant of a shift in social and philosophical environments. It appears that Eastern techniques, *per se*, do not cure drug use; given a change of climate, it cures itself.

The above discussion is not to discredit Wallace and Benson, who are perfectly aware of the deficiencies of their retrospective study and are performing a well-controlled prospective study to replace it. Nor is it to debunk the Great State of Illinois, although, one must confess, the resolution does seem to have been perhaps a trifle over-enthusiastic in its pronouncement. Certainly it is not intended to question the overall value of Transcendental Meditation, though I do feel that TM has more than once endangered its reputation among educated people by prematurely broadcasting scientific findings of tentative caliber. Finally the discussion does not even propose to provide definitive quantitative evidence for the "subculture shift" hypothesis, for my data are subject to some of the same questions of sampling and causality as those of Wallace and Benson. Perhaps what both studies really reveal is one thing: the hazards of attempting to explain the phenomena of youth subcultures on the basis of quantitative results alone. So let us leave now, abandon the numbers and the hypothesizing, and listen, instead to the people themselves, the actual human beings on the road East.

3/ POISON AND PURIFICATION

THE AFTERMATH OF ACID

During a one-month Transcendental Meditation course in August 1972, I got to know another meditator named Jim Mayer, a thin twenty-three-year-old youth with short blond hair, a small neat beard, and deep-set blue eyes. We spent a lot of time together, at dinner, after lectures, and walking to the beach in the misty summer evenings. Often we talked about the events of the day, but Jim liked most to talk about his home near San Antonio, Texas. He lived about forty miles outside of the city in a huge old house with six other meditators. They had been together for more than a year.

"I guess you could call it a commune," he said, "because we share most things in common and do a lot of the work in common. We have one really big room on the first floor where we keep incense burning and have a picture of Maharishi on the wall. That's the room we meditate in together. It's a really nice room. It has a really good atmosphere, and you feel freed from the outside world when you go in there. But most of the other rooms we have separately. We each have our own bedrooms."

"Do you eat together and buy food together?"

"Sometimes, but not completely, because different people are into different food trips there. None of us eats meat, of course, but some are stricter than others. Like Jane, for example, doesn't eat anything that comes from animals, like milk or cheese or eggs or anything. I haven't gotten to that level yet. I still drink milk and so forth. We all eat a lot of stuff made from soybeans. I like that. It makes me feel good to eat things made from soybeans. I just sort of get the feeling that it's something really good for you. There's something really positive about soybeans."

"What is it about soybeans that's positive?"

"Well, I don't know. It just feels good. I feel better after I eat them. I work better and feel more alert and aware during the day. You know, as a matter of fact, I brought some soybean flour to the course to keep in my room, just so that I have something to munch on when I'm hungry.

"Not all of us are into that, though. Like Jack is much more into things like peanut butter and honey. He probably eats too much honey, though. I'm sure it's better than white sugar, but it still seems to me that if you eat too much it must be bad for you. At any rate, I don't eat too much honey myself."

"Where do you get your food?"

"Mostly at one of the organic food stores in town. We'd really like to be able to make our own food, and we've tried it a little bit, but it's really hard to do much farming when you're out in the desert. I mean, it's not exactly a desert, but it's pretty dry."

"So you don't eat any regular supermarket-type foods?"

"Oh God, no, not if I can help it. I mean, it probably doesn't do you any harm to eat a certain amount of it, but if you go on eating that sort of thing month after month and year after year, it's going to build up in you, the poisons and chemicals and additives that are in it. You know, I'm not like some people who absolutely a hundred percent refuse to even touch any regular processed foods. I don't make a big scene if somebody offers me supermarket ice cream or cookies or something like that. But I've been getting more and more careful about processed foods the more I hear. If you let poisons build up in you, it's probably going to be bad for your meditations. Bad for everything in you, for that matter."

"So you're afraid that poisons would build up in you? But your body is capable of metabolizing poisons and getting rid of them, too."

"Some poisons, maybe, but not all of them. I mean, after all, how can you know? Nobody really knows what happens to some of these things when they get into your body. Nobody really knows what they do. Like peanut butter, you know, where they use all these hydrogenated fats and preservatives and stuff, and nicotinic acid and so on. You know, maybe those things are harmless and maybe they're not. But why take the chance? It seems to me me that it's a lot safer to eat something that hasn't been contaminated with things that nature didn't intend to be there in the first place. I always feel sort of uncomfortable any time I eat something like that. Like, I know it probably isn't going to make any difference to do it that one time, but it still makes me a little uncomfortable, you know what I mean?"

"Sure, I do know what you mean, but a lot of people go on eating regular supermarket-type diets every day without seeming to have any bad effects."

"Yeah, sure, I used to eat a diet like that, too. Your body sort of adjusts to it — it sort of becomes accustomed to taking in a certain amount of poison every day that it has to deal with. And you don't even realize the negative effect it's having on you. Like you know Allen, here at the course? Well, he eats a lot of red meat, or at least he did up until the beginning of the course. And of course he couldn't get any here, because they don't serve it. Well, about three days ago, he started going through 'grease withdrawal.' He started having this craving for meat. He'd come back to the room in the afternoon and gross everybody out by saying something like, 'Boy, would I like to have a steak right now!' and he'd sit and lick his lips. Anyway, yesterday it got too much for him, and he went down to the hamburger stand and bought a double cheeseburger. I was with him. After he bought it he stood there and squeezed it, and watched all the juice

ooze out the sides and down over the bottom. He sat there
and caressed the thing for about five minutes before he actually ate it. It was really funny. But it goes to show you —
it's just like drugs. Your body can get hooked on something,
even if it's bad for you. And sometimes it takes quite a long
time to purify your body after it's gotten into something for
a long time."

"Grease withdrawal:" it sounds as bad as going "cold turkey" after
being addicted to heroin. Yet such analogies are ubiquitous in the
conversations of youths throughout all of the Eastern disciplines that
I have known. A universal, central image in their minds is that of *toxicity,* the accumulation of vaguely defined evil substances in body and
mind. Usually they imply a chronic process, a creeping, insidious
poisoning which is barely perceptible and therefore all the more dangerous. A similar theme appeared in a later conversation when Jim and
I got to talking about drugs:

"None of the people in our house in Texas ever uses drugs
anymore. Jane and Dennis used to smoke grass a little bit
maybe a year ago, but now they've stopped completely. The
more you meditate, the more you get to realize that even using
drugs a little bit can leave negative influences that last a long
time. You become more sensitive to drug effects. You begin
to see how incredibly much they've been doping up your
mind. Like, you know, when I was in college, I was taking
drugs all the time, every single day, and my mind just got
dulled to it, you know? I was so deep into the whole thing
that I couldn't even recognize the bad influences that drugs
had on my thinking. I didn't really know what it felt like to
feel really good and really awake, so I had nothing to compare it to when I was in college, if you see what I mean."

"Yeah, so what's it like now that you've been meditating?"

"Oh well, now that I've been meditating for a year and
haven't taken drugs, everything's different. It's as if my
body and mind are cleaned out, and they're *still* cleaning
out even now. The thing which really shows that is how
much more sensitive you get to things once your system becomes really cleaned out. Like last month three of us
from the house split a single can of beer — one little twelve-

ounce can — and we all got smashed, just on that miniscule
amount of alcohol, because our bodies had become so much
more purified and more sensitive to drugs. And if I was to
eat a piece of steak now, I'll bet I'd get really sick, because
all of the red meat influences have gone out of my body now."

Another even more familiar expression of the poison theme was
Jim's description of driving to work:

"I wish I didn't have to work in San Antonio, even though
it's part time. When I drive in there in the morning, particularly when it's a calm, windless day, you can see a cloud of
pollution, sort of a haze, hanging over the city. I always
think to myself, 'God, I'm going to be working inside that
cloud for the next six hours!' and I almost feel sick. It
bothers me. I feel a lot better when I'm outside the boundaries of the city and driving back toward the house."

"Is it desertlike, where your house is?"

"No, not a desert, but it's pretty barren. I like it. I
like the feel of being out there."

Jim's concern with purity, not just in the sense of the mental and
spiritual purity he seeks, but in the concrete sense of the food he eats
and the air he breathes, is typical of hundreds of youths I have met in
various Eastern disciplines. Many, in fact, have a far greater preoccupation with it than he, and even more rigorous standards for avoiding
adverse physical and spiritual influences. I have met a surprising number who, like him, live in remote, "clean" areas: a cleared patch of
forest in British Columbia, a teepee in central Oregon, islands such as
Martha's Vineyard and Cape Breton, and, very frequently, barren
desert areas such as Arizona, New Mexico, and parts of southern California. The Lama Foundation, for example, a well-known ashram
founded by Baba Ram Dass (the former Dr. Richard Alpert of LSD
fame) is located in a desolate part of New Mexico.

It is not surprising to find an emphasis on purity among those on the
road East; the great Western religions, for that matter, grew up in des-
erts as well. But what of this acute awareness of poison, the scrupulous
avoidance of negative influences? To some extent, surely, it represents
a reaction to real danger, but how much does the sense of creeping
toxicity symbolize something deeper?

In talking about the poison theme with many youths in various disciplines, I was constantly impressed by the number of their references to former drug use. A great many of them were scared out of drug use by taking an overdose of something, seeing a friend do so, or more frequently, because they began to fear a gradual dilapidation of their physical and mental health. An example of the latter case is a twenty-six-year-old named Harold who is now a member of the Nicherin Shoshu sect of Buddhism:

"I didn't have much trouble with drugs, or so I thought, up until about the last year when we lived in New York. In those days we were doing everything we could get our hands on, but especially amphetamines — shooting amphetamines. I spent about ninety-nine percent of my time in the area of one block in New York, and most of it in just one apartment. And after awhile it got so that I was really sick. I'd get up in the morning and the first thing I'd want to do would be to throw up. Sometimes I used to throw up two or three times, and then, after my stomach was emptied out, I'd go on having the dry heaves for hours. And it got so that just looking at food would make me really sick — even thinking about food. That went on for about two months and after awhile I just started getting disgusted with the whole thing. I got the feeling that I wasn't bouncing back from taking drugs like I did in the old days, like I was slowly going downhill. Like my whole body and my mind were slowly wiping out. And one day this guy I knew came by and wanted me to come to the meeting and chant, so I did. That first time I didn't get particularly turned on by the chanting, but the people were all so *alive*, and I suddenly felt that I had been really wrecking my brain and that I just needed to get out of it. And so maybe a month later I went back to another meeting, and then I suddenly began to really get turned on to it. Now that I've been chanting for six months I just can't believe the change that's come over me. It's like a whole new world. In fact, I went back and talked to one of my friends from New York and now he's chanting too. It's really true, you know, you really do get what you wish for when you chant."

Harold's story is more graphic than most in that he actually became physically sick for a period of time. But a larger number of former drug users recall a vague fear that something was happening to their minds, an uncomfortable suspicion that their awareness, their sense of self-control, or even their sanity was being steadily but imperceptibly undermined by drugs, particularly LSD. And this, though subtle, was ultimately much more terrifying than physical deterioration. For some, the fear was quite conscious and could often be traced back to a particular moment of panic. But for the majority, the fear of poisoning built up on an unconscious level and was never specifically attributed to LSD or other drug use, but instead generalized to the world as a whole.

This merits further elaboration, because it is often an important basis for the poison fear. Its magnitude is difficult to appreciate if one is not familiar with the vicissitudes of the LSD experience. To begin with, LSD can be a very humbling experience, particularly for the user who highly values his rationality and intellectuality. It is profoundly unnerving to discover that an invisibly small amount of a chemical can utterly dissolve mental structures and organization that one had always regarded as a given, as something automatic, reliable, indestructible. Many users, particularly older ones, emerge from successive trips with an increased, though often unconscious, sense of their own mutability and fragility, with the realization that it is possible for the mind, without warning, to abruptly do something totally foreign to what the rest of the organism anticipates or desires. And if the mind is so vulnerable, the unconscious reasoning may continue, what other invisible contaminants might be compromising it — an unsuspected vitamin deficiency? Hexachlorophene? An artificial food color and flavor? Or perhaps a nonchemical poison: stress, "bad vibrations" from one's neighbors, "negative energy," or a lifestyle that is unnatural in some way. Although the chain of reasoning is usually far below the threshold of conscious cognition, it comes close to the surface in statements such as this from a Buddhist meditator in Ohio: "I really liked tripping the times I did it in California, but looking back on it, it makes me sort of uncomfortable. I don't like that sensation of being out of control, and I think that those times with LSD are one of the reasons that maybe I've been more careful of myself since." Or a high-school student who has become a follower of Guru Maharaj Ji: "One thing that taking drugs taught me is that negative influences can last a long time without you even knowing they're there. You learn that you have to watch out for them."

But to me the most moving account was from Jim Mayer. He told it to me on one of our last late-night walks, near the end of the course in August:

"Well, I'll tell you what happened to me. It's sort of a scarey story, even to tell it now. It was in my senior year at Columbia, in February. It was a cold, drizzly night in New York, and I was feeling really depressed. Most of all, I wanted a girl, I guess, but my girl was two hundred miles away and I couldn't see her. So the next best thing to do was to get high. I had taken acid twice in the last month and I didn't want to do it again right away. I'd done methedrine a few times, too. Anyhow, I was taking this anthropology course and I had been reading about how the Indians in Central America took belladonna and had hallucinations. And for some reason, I remembered that Contac cold pills had belladonna in them. So I went down to an all-night drugstore — it was about midnight by this time — and bought twenty Contac capsules. Then I brought them home and opened up twelve of them and ground up all the little time capsules inside with a spoon, so that I'd get the full dose all at once. And then I took the whole thing, all twelve capsules full.

"I felt fine for about forty minutes and then I began to notice that I could see some colors in front of my eyes, and I thought, 'Hey, this is going to be good!' But right after that I began to feel this headache coming on, and it got worse and worse until my head was pounding. Then I decided to go in- to the bathroom and look at myself in the mirror. So I did, and then it was just incredibly horrifying, because my face was white, just as white as a piece of paper, and my neck and chest were covered with bright red blotches, red as red paint. And the headache was getting worse. I reached down and took my pulse, and just standing there, it was 180 beats a minute! Then I started to get really scared. I tried to vomit but I couldn't. So I paced around my room for awhile, maybe five minutes. It seemed like an hour. I was really afraid to go to the infirmary for fear that they would tell, you know, that people would find out about the whole thing, maybe my parents or the dean or something. So I sat down and tried to sort of will my body to quiet down. Then I took my pulse

again, and it was going so fast that I could hardly even count
it. I didn't even dare count it, but finally I did and it was 250.
And I suddenly realized that if I didn't get to the hospital I
was going to die. You know, that this was the real thing and
I was really going to die if I didn't get there. Or maybe I was
going to die anyway, before I even got out of my room to go
there, like a brain hemorrhage or something, like maybe in
the next three seconds I'd suddenly have a white flash behind
my eyes and then suddenly go paralyzed and blind, and just
be a vegetable for the next fifty years.

"So, anyhow a couple of friends took me down to the hospital, and when they took my blood pressure there the mercury
went off the top of the machine — it was over 300. So then
they gave me a shot of stuff to bring my blood pressure down
and pumped my stomach and then gave me a whopping dose
of barbiturates or something or other that knocked me out
for about eighteen hours. When I finally came to, there was
this psychiatrist sitting beside my bed, wanting to know why
I had tried to commit suicide. I explained to him that I hadn't
been trying to commit suicide, but that I was only trying to
get high, and that for some weird reason, I had just decided
that it would be safe to take that much stuff.

"Well, after I recovered from it all — the headache wasn't
completely gone for a week — and I thought back on it, the
thing that really freaked me out to think of was not that I
had almost died, or not even that maybe I had done permanent damage to my brain, but that I could have made such a
weird mistake in judgment in the first place. I was smart
enough to know that there were all kinds of other ingredients
in Contac that would be dangerous if you took them in an
overdose, but somehow my mind just ignored that fact on
that night. And that's what was really scarey — the idea that
my mind could just run away from me and do something
freaky like that without warning. I guess it was just a long-
term influence of the acid I had taken a month earlier, some
sort of delayed-action thing, at least that's what I assume it
was.

"I took a few drugs on a few occasions after that time, but

that was sort of the end of the drug scene for me. I think
I've never lost the fear from that time, because I can still feel
it coming out now, three years later, when I tell you the story.
I think I'm still on the rebound from that fear, if you know
what I mean."

Only a minority of meditators exited precipitously from the drug
world through a terrifying experience like Jim's. But many more, conditioned by a long series of lesser traumas, retain a residue of unconscious
poison-fear in their new lives. Much of their preoccupation with physical and mental health, their emphasis on purity of body and mind, and
their hyperesthesia for contamination in the environment, can be traced
to this.

IT'S NOT SAFE JUST TO LIVE HERE

But of course the fear of poison also has a more immediate and fac-
tual basis, stemming from our national awakening to the dangers of pollution and food additives. Meditators are hardly unique, and probably
not even the most extreme, in such fears, but their particular response
to environmental pollution is distinctive. Listen to the following inter-
change among a group of followers of Guru Maharaj Ji on the subject
of fasting:

"I'm really hungry. I missed breakfast this morning
again."

"Sometimes it's good to miss a meal now and then. I
wouldn't feel bad about having missed breakfast. Your digestive tract sometimes needs a rest so that it can clean out
all the poisons that have built up in your body."

"Well, I tried fasting once for that reason, but after the
third day I felt sort of sick and really weak."

"Did you get lots of rest while you were fasting?"

"No more than usual. I just went about my daily activities as usual."

"Well, that was your problem, then. Your body has to
do a lot of work to eliminate all of the poisons that have
built up, so you have to get lots and lots of rest during a fast
to allow your body to have all its energies to work on the
poisons."

"I tried fasting, too," said a girl, "and I didn't have any trouble while I was fasting, but on the fifth day when I started eating again, I got diarrhea."

"Yes, but getting diarrhea is not necessarily bad because it's just an expression of your body's work of getting rid of the poison. Getting a cold can be good in some ways, too, because coughing and blowing your nose and so forth can also help your body to get rid of poisons that have built up."

I also recall a conversation with an Ananda Marga meditator from Chicago:

"I wonder if there's a good chiropractor around here," he said. "You've got something wrong with you?" I asked.

"Yeah, I've got these pains in my back. I've had them on and off for a month now. It gets worse when I breathe. I'm pretty sure I know what it is, but . . ."

"What is it?"

"Well, I think I have a little knot of poison accumulated underneath here," he said, pointing to a thoracic vertebra, "and I think some of it has flowed to *here* and down to *here*. I can feel it. It's little knots of poison that I haven't been able to get rid of."

"Where did the poison come from in the first place?"

"I don't know. All different places, maybe. There's no way you can tell where you pick it up."

Such accounts are not at all uncommon, nor are they confined only to a few Eastern disciplines. For youths such as these, poison is not an abstract possibility, anticipated as a potential danger. It is an immediate, omnipresent threat, requiring constant vigilance here and now. The poisonous influences are not even readily identifiable; they float unrecognized in the environment, colorless, odorless, already beginning to take their toll long before they are recognized.

A final, more detailed example is a dinner-table conversation last spring at a commune in western Massachusetts. Four of the five speakers here are Transcendental Meditators, but with certain translations, the conversation might well have occurred among several other groups on the road East, anywhere in the country.

"This fish is good. I haven't eaten fish in a long time. What kind is it?"

"It's scrod."

"Isn't there supposed to be mercury in scrod?"

"I don't know. I haven't seen anything about mercury recently in the news."

"They wrote a report, didn't they? Claiming that the danger was over, or something, or that the amount of mercury you were getting in fish was not harmful?"

"Any amount of mercury might be harmful. How can anybody know? How do they know it doesn't have some effect on your consciousness? Just because they can't measure something on the gross level doesn't mean it doesn't do anything on a subtle level, as Maharishi would say."

"I get the feeling that the whole mercury thing's been suppressed. I wonder if there isn't somebody who's making an incredible amount of money on fish who paid somebody off to put some pressure on people to keep the publicity down."

"It makes you wonder, doesn't it?"

"Yeah, it's just like those things where big food companies were adding something to food and using their power to keep the government from releasing information about it."

"Or they publish an article 'proving' that it's safe, and everybody believes it but nobody really knows whether it's true or not."

"Yeah, there's no way you can fight it or investigate it even, because there's no way you can have all the facts."

"Unless you could be about ten thousand Ralph Naders working at the same time."

"I'll bet that there are probably a lot of people who could do that kind of investigating, you know, who have the knowledge to separate truth from fiction in something like that. But they all get off in their labs or someplace and get going on what they're interested in, and their talents are lost."

Later in the conversation, "But one thing Maharishi says, though, is that as you evolve, your body gets better and better at distinguishing what's good for it and what's bad for it. When you reach a certain level your body will simply be able to tell whether something is bad for you or not."

"I wonder if when we reach cosmic consciousness we'll

be able to taste whether there's mercury in fish or not?"

"Well, I don't think you'd necessarily be able to *taste* it, but you'd just get so that you didn't like to eat scrod, so that you just didn't enjoy it anymore."

"I sort of lost my taste for red meat like that. It wasn't as though one day I decided to give it up. I just gradually got so that I didn't like it as much anymore, and after awhile, I wasn't eating it at all."

"I don't know. Maybe people in cosmic consciousness really can taste something like mercury. Because as you evolve, the system becomes more and more purified, and so your sensitivity to impurities gets greater. Like they've done scientific studies that show that meditators develop better and better visual and hearing senses, and I'll bet the same applies for taste."

Again, slightly later, "The thing that really freaks me out is that they can put chemicals into food that can fool your body into thinking that they taste good when actually all you're eating is a bunch of chemicals."

"Yeah, Like did you even try to read the list of ingredients on one of those substitutes for coffee cream? It's incredible. After about the first two, I don't even know what all the rest of them *are*. Like what's that poly—, poly—?"

"Polysorbate 80?" I asked.

"Yeah, what's that?"

"I haven't the foggiest idea."

"But you studied nutrition at medical school, didn't you?"

"Yes, but they never taught us what polysorbate 80 was. I'm pretty sure it's safe, but I really don't know."

"Well, there's a good example. You're going to be a doctor, which means that you're supposed to be able to advise people about the right things to eat, and if *you* don't know what that stuff is, how's anybody else supposed to know?"

"But the thing that I think is even worse," said another, "is that they can get people to like a product through advertising. You know, that they can actually persuade people that they *like* something when they haven't even tried it. That happens all the time when they *create* a market for something."

"Yeah, that's really amazing, how people can be persuaded that they *need* something that they actually don't need. You have gotten along without one for the last fifty years, but you need one now. And people suddenly start to think that they actually *do* need whatever it is."

"You know, that's one of the first things that happened to me after I started to meditate. I got so that I couldn't stand things like that. They began to seem so ridiculous to me."

"That's true. The more you meditate, the more you get so that that sort of thing doesn't affect you anymore."

"I wonder how much difference it would make in how fast you evolved if you went on leading exactly the same life, eating the same things, and so on, as before you started meditating?" I asked.

"Well, a lot of meditators do that, and they still evolve."

"The thing is that as they meditate, their lives get purer in such an automatic way that they're not aware of how much they've changed."

"Yeah. That what's so nice about it. You don't *have* to change your life! You just meditate, and take it as it comes, and your life changes automatically!"

"But I'm sure it's true that if you have a purer life to start with, you evolve faster."

"The thing which is really nice is when you reach a high enough level of consciousness, you get so that bad influences just bounce off you. Like you could eat some fish with mercury in it, and your body would immediately reject the mercury. Just reject it!"

"I really like that idea, too. It really appealed to me when I first heard it at a lecture. The idea that when your body is at a really high level of consciousness, it's like rubber, and poisons just bounce off it. Like you could even take drugs if you wanted to and it wouldn't leave any effect on your body."

I have greatly condensed this conversation, preserving mainly those fragments containing references to poison and purification. Some of the statements are not much different from what one might hear at many other dinner tables, among people who were neither meditators nor former drug users. But the conversation is distinctive in two respects. First, the meditators display a greater *degree* of concern than most other groups. In fact, youths in Eastern disciplines are more sensitive to the implications of environmental poison than any other large group of youths I have known except the more extreme organic food eaters, who overlap so heavily with the Eastern group as to be barely distinguishable. Secondly, the meditators have a particular *response* to the poison threat which separates them from others. To appreciate this, we must consider a cluster of themes which emerge in the above conversation, themes which recur elsewhere in this book in contexts other than poison, and which may well seem familiar to the reader already.

The first theme — common in our society — is that of an *uncaring authority figure*: the corporation which suppresses nasty evidence about a food additive, the government which hastily placates the public with an irresponsible report, the expert who declines to use his expertise for the public good. The meditators rarely depict the authority as actively and deliberately malicious, as some consumer or political groups might, but simply as unconcerned with the welfare of its subjects. And although meditators' distrust for such authority has an indisputable basis in fact, the authority image also has a compelling resemblance to the distant father figure which I have previously described in the family backgrounds of drug users. This image of the father — uncaring, but not actively malicious — if it is true, is not unique to meditators, but it is certainly pervasive among them.

A second theme, still general but a bit more specific to youths in Eastern disciplines, might be called *poisoning the mind*, as suggested by the idea that one can be manipulated unawares by scientific advertising techniques, brainwashed by a calculated bombardment of messages. It is like the post-LSD state described earlier in its implication that one may be persuaded to do something without having been aware of the persuasion process. Again, it is more frightening because it cannot be recognized in advance.

Another theme is that of *complexity*, the implication that things are too complicated for the average person to deal with, that unless one could be ten thousand Ralph Naders, or had a panel of consulting experts on hand at every moment, one could never be absolutely sure of being safe. Here the meditators begin to take a much different tack from some other groups, saying that since no one can acquire enough expertise to simultaneously fight all the dangers, it is foolish to attack "the system" on its own grounds.

Instead, the meditators have a distinctive alternative that is hinted at in the above conversation. It might be summarized by the statements, "It's not safe just to live here. You have to consciously start on a program to take care of yourself." Distrusting the dim authorities whom they sense at the controls of the environment, wary of insidious influences it may have on their minds, and confessing their inability to combat the system, they have chosen an Eastern discipline, in part, as a sort of umbrella against the poison around them. For many, a protective, infinitely caring new father figure replaces the old, a life of serenity and purity insulates against noxious mental influences, and a simple program of physical and mental hygiene reduces the complexities of coping with the modern environment. Regardless of the particular technique they follow, those on the road East evolve an increasing sense of immunity to the sepsis they perceive in the surrounding environment. And for a greater number, as for the Transcendental Meditators quoted above, this includes a literal belief that they are gaining resistance to actual chemical poisons as well as the intangible ones.

4/ FROM THE FILLMORE TO THE FARM

THE LIGHT SHOW AND BEYOND

Ellie is a twenty-five-year old who lives on a farm in Maine, together with her husband, John, and two eighteen-year-old boys who have become more or less permanent residents of the place. For several years, all four have been doing Kriya Yoga, taught by an excellent but unpublicized teacher in Boston whom they met through friends. Ellie is a striking figure, very tall, with straight brown hair extending almost to her waist, and all the more imposing in the ankle-length dresses she often wears.

I first met her at an outdoor rock concert in southern New Hampshire, several summers ago, when we both were sitting in a large circle of people eating lunch on the lawn. I was innocently devouring a cheese sandwich when an unfamiliar female voice said out of the blue, "Do you realize that what you're eating is made from the stomachs of *dead cows*? Don't you find that DISGUSTING?"

I was rather intimidated because she was a good two inches taller than I and looked very disapproving. But in the conversation that ensued, I quickly lost my fear and found her to be a warm, good-hearted person. Later in the conversation, John began to join in. He was equally friendly, but more taciturn, more reserved, with a distant look in his eyes, and a visage buried beneath long black hair and a weatherbeaten beard.

During the course of the afternoon, we got to talking about past

times: Ellie had met John in Haight-Ashbury in San Francisco, where
she had been since 'way back in 1965, the golden days of the oldtime
hippies. She and John had lived together there from the summer of
1967, when Haight-Ashbury first began to be invaded by tourists, until
late 1968, when crime and heroin had caused it to decay.

Both had many stories to tell about the San Francisco scene, but
most of all I remember Ellie's lyrical description of concerts at the Fillmore Auditorium, the mecca of acid rock in the Western Hemisphere,
as she saw them in the old days:

> "We used to go to the Fillmore about once a week. We
> heard all the groups there — everybody — long before they
> became known to the rest of the country. It used to be a
> cool feeling to go there, because you had a feeling of being
> at the throbbing center of the universe. It was like the
> point from which radiated out the sounds that moved the
> whole world . . . .
>
> "You'd get stoned out of your mind on grass, or sometimes
> do acid, and go, and the place would be jammed with people,
> and dark and smokey with the smell of all the people jammed
> in there. And up at the front, blazing in light, would be the
> group who was going to play, with their huge piles of ampli-
> fiers and electronics all facing you like a wall of power. Some-
> times when I was stoned I used to go up to the stage and just
> groove on the electronics, on all the knobs and lights. You
> could look at it and just get into it until you could feel the
> electricity zapping around along all the wires and the tubes
> pulsating in time to the music . . . .
>
> "And when they played, you could feel the pressure of the
> sound, like walls of pressure hitting you as they moved out
> from the stage. The whole thing would just blow out your
> circuits and give you the feeling that you were one with the
> sound. There were a lot of times when I would just groove
> on that feeling instead of on the music itself. Just the
> feeling of being swallowed up into an electronic womb, and
> then being left there for four hours until you were finally
> released back into the real world again."

John added, "That was really what those times used to be
like for a lot of people. A lot of people grooved on that. I

remember somebody once said something like that hippies preferred the electrical to the mechanical. And I can understand why, because the electrical was faster, and more modern. People just got into that sort of thing."

"What has changed? You both talk about it like a thing of the past," I said.

Ellie pondered for awhile, then said, "What happened is that people just started to burn out, sort of like the way you'd tell about a speed freak being burned out. The tubes just died in their brains. People just began to realize something wasn't right, I guess.

"It's funny what happened to me. The last few times I went to the Fillmore, I guess it must have been 1969, I used to fall asleep on the floor every time I went. It got so that I'd get inside and there'd be this super-decibel music playing, and I'd lie down and the next thing I knew I'd been asleep for half an hour right in the middle of the most impossible place to fall asleep in the world. And I know about three other people that that happened to, also, It was just your body saying 'no!' to the whole bag, sort of the wisdom of your mind telling you that this thing wasn't good for you anymore."

"You mean a feeling that you had lost your ability to tolerate it?"

"No, not really. Like here we are at a rock concert right now, and we're still enjoying it. It's not as if I can't hack it anymore, if that's what you're trying to say. It was realizing that the whole thing wasn't positive for your body or for your mind, or I should say for your whole person because your body and mind are really the same thing anyway. People just got to realize that they were burning themselves out, that they'd just come to the end of that phase of their lives, and that it was just piling more and more negative energy on their bodies.

"Maybe it has something to do with growing older, in a way, now that I think of it. When you're a teen-ager that sort of thing bounces off you, or you can absorb a lot of it without feeling anything from it. And then gradually you get so

that you don't absorb it as easily. That may have something
to do with it."

"So it was around 1969 that you began to move away from
that sort of thing?"

"Yes. And then it must have been in the beginning of 1970
that John and I met our teacher in Boston and started getting
into yoga. And then of course everything began to change."

Ellie's account I think describes very beautifully a sequence that has
been followed by many on the road East. They began, in their younger
years, in the carefree grass-and-acid years of the late sixties, by regarding technology, without fear, as a munificent mother. Not only could
it feed and clothe them for free — as it often did — but it offered a
whole garden of special effects, a Coney Island of entertainment: electric bands, light shows, big hi-fi systems, and most significantly, an endless array of drug experiences — the constant novelty of LSD, the fantastic colors of mescaline, the roller-coaster ride of DMT, and more.
Speed and constant change, pictured by their elders as evils of our age,
the hippies welcomed: persistently they sought new cities, new experiences, new friends and lovers, new fads and stars, the electrical as
opposed to the mechanical, and, ultimately, the experience of sensory
saturation, as in taking LSD and going to the Fillmore. And not merely sensory saturation, but sensory overload, the state implicit in that
pervasive phrase, "to blow the mind." Did Nirvana lie beyond that saturation threshold, many wondered, or merely the rubble of a psyche
that temporarily could not remain intact?

It was Donovan, one of the earliest singers of the acid era, who first
introduced many of us to the phrase "blow your mind" in a searing
song, "Sunshine Superman," nearly ten years ago. But later, in his deli-
cate album, "A Gift from a Flower to a Garden," he was one of the
first to see the danger of overacceleration in a famous line, "The whole
wide world is taking too much Methedrine."

Significantly, Donovan became an early practitioner of Transcendental Meditation and is pictured on the back of that album sitting with
Maharishi Mahesh Yogi.

The same trend, from technology-as-mother to technology-as-mon-
ster, appears in the songs of many other rock singers, including those
fathers of the Fillmore, the Jefferson Airplane. Described on their first
LP as a "jet-aged sound," they achieved national prominence in 1967

with their superb second album, "Surrealistic Pillow." It is a classic of
the light-show style, evidenced more in the blinding impact of its music
than in the words of a particular song. The second side begins with
"Three-fifths of a Mile in Ten Secc ids," continues through the hallucinogenic excursion of "White Rabbit," and ends with a facetious, but
faintly infatuated, ode to technology, "Plastic Fantastic Lover":

> Her neon mouth with premitsal smile, nothing but
> > an electric sign
> You could say she has an individual style, she's
> > a part of a colorful time.
> Super-sealed lady, chrome-colored clothes you
> > wear 'cause you have no other
> But I suppose no one knows you're my plastic
> > fantastic lover . . . .

But by 1970, in "Volunteers," they sing "The Farm":

> Yes, it's good livin' on the farm
> Ah, so good livin' on the farm
> Yes, it's good livin' on the farm . . . .

And "Wooden Ships," in all rock music perhaps the most moving portrait of technological society as a malignant thing. The song equally un-
derscores the previous chapter, for it contains gripping imagery of poison
and purification, and the symbolic implication that the only safety lies
in an escape to a new life:

> Black sails knifing through the pitchblende night
> Away from the radioactive landmass madness
> From the silver-suited people searching out
> Uncontaminated food and shelter on the shores
> No glowing metal on our ship of wood only
> Free happy crazy people naked in the universe
> WE SPEAK EARTH TALK
> GO RIDE THE MUSIC
>
> If you smile at me you know I will understand
> Cause that is something everybody everywhere does
> In the same language
> I can see by your coke my friend that you're from the other side
> There's just one thing I got to know
> Can you tell me please who won
> You must try some of my purple berries

I been eating them for six or seven weeks now
Haven't got sick once
Probably keep us both alive

Wooden ships on the water very free and easy
Easy you know the way it's supposed to be
Silver people on the shoreline leave us be
Very free and easy . . . .

Go and take a sister by her hand
Lead her far from this foreign land
Somewhere where we might laugh again
We are leaving
You don't need us

For many of those on the road East, it was only a few years from the chrome-clothed lady to the silver-suited people, from a brief but intense affair with the electronic age to a rejection of technology and all it represents. The process of "burning out," as Ellie aptly described it, paralleled disenchantment with drugs, and as the aftermath of LSD created a rebound hypersensitivity to poison, so the aftermath of the light-show era, of the search for new thrills and new stimulation, produced an enhanced distaste for complexity, artificiality, speed and stress.

DOES YOUR NUMBER MATCH?

But there is nothing new in the rejection of artificiality, the trend toward nature. Everybody is doing it. You can buy natural ice cream, natural soft drinks, vitamins obtained entirely from natural sources, even natural cigarettes (imagine — nature's own tar and nicotine with no ugly chemicals added!). A glance at the billboards will show that technology, characteristically, has been quick to cash in on the back-to-nature trip. It is already being digested, already fad-ized. What, then, is so special about meditators?

First, as with fear of poison, it is a difference of degree. Those in Eastern disciplines are among the most concerned, most serious about the deleterious effects of complexity and artificiality. The concern permeates every aspect of their lives. Witness a conversation I had with a Buddhist in Vermont:

"Why are you so careful to avoid refined sugar?"

"Because it robs your body of B vitamins."

"Well, yes, that's true, but that's what B vitamins are made for. Any food that has energy in it automatically has to use up B vitamins to be used by your body."

"Well, maybe, but refined sugar doesn't give you back any of the B vitamins that it robs. If you eat unrefined sugar, then at least you're getting vitamins in addition to the sugar. But you're right. The best thing to do would be to eat no sugar of any kind, and just eat foods exactly the way nature made them."

"Well, I see what you mean, but after all, why should it do you any *harm* to eat refined sugar? You're getting plenty of B vitamins from other sources. Surely you have enough to spare to handle a little refined sugar."

"Well, yes, that's technically true, I'm sure, but it still doesn't make me want to eat refined sugar. It's just, I guess it's just that refined sugar is so — artificial."

Another example, from a Transcendental Meditator in Washington state named Butch, is a dream that he recounted to me the morning after it happened. Although I will not attempt to interpret the entire dream, the elements of fearful complexity and artificiality are obvious.

"I came to the world from somewhere else and it was all very different. I was looking for my girl, Susan. I was in a tall building with hundreds of staircases going back and forth all the way to the top. It was all very modern and white. And then I suddenly knew that you had to have a ticket, some kind of card with a number on it, in order to be on earth. And they would *process* you if you didn't have a ticket."

"Process?"

"Yes, they'd make you into a member of their world, sort of. And I was really afraid of it. And I was trying to save Susan from all of this. She had become one of them. She sympathized with their ways, and I just wanted to get hold of her and tell her I loved her so she wouldn't put me aside."

"And then?"

"I ran out and people were screaming something like, 'The numbers don't correspond on his card!' And I ran

down this ramp, trying to escape, and I came into sort of a little park with cement benches and cement shrubbery painted
green. And then I caught Susan and I was pleading with her
and she kept going away, but I finally convinced her and
she said, 'Okay, if my husband in Vietnam doesn't mind.' "

During the week prior to the dream, Butch had been trying, without
much success, to persuade the real Susan to take up Transcendental
Meditation. She did not in fact have a husband in Vietnam, nor was
there anything else to associate her with the war. Possibly the dream
husband symbolizes, in part, her unwillingness to break with more conventional American values to the degree that Butch has.

Not only are meditators more afraid of the artificial, but they are
also distinguished by their emphasis on *discipline*. This reflects a discovery that is at once trivial and profound, namely that happiness must
be worked for and cannot be bought. To some readers this may seem
the most obvious of clichés, yet it may be that for many youths on the
road East it represented a difficult discovery.

First, as in the case of the hallucinogenic drug culture, young meditators were brought up in affluent homes. Few of them came from
lower- or working-class areas, and almost none grew up in real poverty.
Correlated with this is the fact that certainly less than 3 percent of them
are Black, and probably less than 1 percent. Most of them experienced
a childhood that was more comfortable physically than that enjoyed by
the vast majority of other children on the planet. They never wrestled
with fears about food, clothing, and shelter; rarely did they experience
danger, pain, or any significant degree of material deprivation. As a result, they bore a minimum of responsibility. They grew up in an atmosphere where self-denial and self-discipline had become, in comparison
with the lives of other children, almost obsolete.

Superimposed on this background were the surrounding culture's
definitions of happiness. In television advertisements, they watched
housewives ecstatically examining their hands after using a new brand
of dishwashing soap, teenagers finally succeeding with the opposite sex
after changing their deodorant, poolside guests discovering the host's
brand of beer with surprised delight. All the messages read that happiness was prompt and purchasable, the sum of manmade pleasures; that
if one felt just miserable, the solution was to change brands.

Later, they absorbed playboy images of men with plush pads or plush

yachts, swimming pools and sports cars, surrounded by doting females
(they were materials, too). Obtain the appropriate accoutrements, the
pictures implied, and the happiness followed automatically.

Finally, the drug culture was merely an extension of the same definition of pleasure, the ultimate in immediate, material solutions. Giv-
en that background, it was a giant step for such youths to stop and
say that there was something wrong, an error, in the fast-and-easy definition of happiness. But perhaps it was an inevitable step; they had
had their fill of the artificial alternative.

They emerged singularly wary of the artificial, with the sense that
anything quick and materialistic was, by definition, fake. It was at
this point that many of them looked to the Orient. An Eastern discipline was eminently natural; unlike mechanical techniques such as
scientology and alpha-wave conditioning, it required nothing but the
individual's own mind and body. As yoga exercises can be performed
in a bare room without bars, swings, or other gimmicks, so the mental techniques are based on the simplest things: the sound of a mantra, the ebb and flow of one's breathing. And though the techniques
are natural and easy, none proposes to be quick in offering fulfillment.
All require months and years of time, and all demand self-discipline.
Not discipline in the cough-medicine sense that it has to be unpleasant to be good for you (a common misinterpretation which we will
discuss in detail later), but discipline as an uplifting thing, a thing which
gives form and structure to life, which gives a more solid and permanent species of happiness.

The straightforward, well-defined routine of following an Eastern
discipline, of meditating or chanting each morning and evening, of
doing yoga exercises for thirty minutes a day, or of associated disciplines such as sleeping more regularly, caring for diet, or doing physical work on a farm, has filled a void that many youths felt in their
old lives. Many even went on to add new little disciplines that were
not officially required for their techniques: sleeping facing east, ob-
serving silence once a month, doing regular work for their group, or
even going to an ashram — a spiritual community — for a period of
time each year.

The value of discipline and the avoidance of artificiality are well
expressed by a girl named Teresa whom I met in California. She
lives permanently in an ashram type of community:

"There are many forms of yoga, and they all contribute
to your spiritual development. But the core of it all is
Karma Yoga, which is just the yoga of work, just living
your life through the day. It's doing the ordinary tasks of
ordinary life like chopping wood and carrying water. And
that simple yoga is more important than anything else . . .

"Before I came here, I was into a very heavy kind of
scene in college. Not much different from what other people did in college, I guess, but constantly doing all different
kinds of things, never settling down. It was a scene in which
I was never really there. I was always thinking about what
I was going to do next, and dissatisfied with what I was doing at the time. Like studying and thinking about a movie
I was going to that night. I was always looking beyond the
present and into the future for something better.

"Now that I've been here for awhile, there's been an
amazing change, just because I've been here, in the present,
doing real things. I couldn't believe how much of a difference that has made in my life!"

Meditators like Teresa, who add to their Eastern technique a life-
discipline, a discipline of *Karma Yoga*, are usually the ones who become most firmly committed to the East, and most certain that they
have advanced in spiritual development and happiness.

A digression is appropriate here. The uplifting effect of the discipline is so dramatic for many meditators that one is prompted to
wonder if perhaps the Eastern technique *per se* is irrelevant, and it is
only the discipline surrounding it that works the change. No answer
can be given; one would have to perform the difficult experiment of
collecting two matched groups of youths who are on the point of taking up an Eastern discipline, then teaching one group a bogus technique and the other the real thing. The bogus technique would have
to require exactly the same daily routine, the same discipline, as the
real one. All other variables would have to be constant: those in the
control group would have to experience the same immersion in the
meditator subculture, have the same opportunity to discipline all other
aspects of their lives, and have no way of finding out from their friends
that the technique they were using was a placebo. Even allowing
that one could perform such an experiment, and assuming that one

possessed some unimpeachable method to quantify "improvement in life" a year or two later, the results would still be in question because there would be no way to perform the experiment blind. Surely the *bona fide* Eastern technique would have to be taught by a legitimate teacher, rather than a hastily briefed scientist (most pro-meditation people would discard the results otherwise), and to avoid confounding variables, he would have to teach the bogus technique as well.

In this or any other teacher-trainee design, there is no way that one could even begin to rule out subliminal cues from the teacher as to whether the technique being transmitted was real or false. Finally, assuming for argument's sake that the experiment could somehow be properly performed, suppose that roughly equal improvements were found in both meditators and controls? One could not be sure that the bogus technique was totally without merit, a genuine placebo. Nor could one confidently generalize the negative results to any other Eastern technique; the experiment would have to be repeated for each in turn.

The quantitative approach again proved hazardous; for such reasons I have based this book on the technique of participant-observation, and have rarely proposed to be quantitative or evaluative in my conclusions. Lacking data, I have avoided pronouncements as to whether Eastern techniques "work" or not. But in regard to the discipline versus technique question, I shall briefly lay out, for those interested, my own observations and beliefs.

I believe that newfound self-discipline alone is a source of great happiness for most youths who seriously enter it. My basis for this is that I have met many youths who emerged from the drug world and adopted a new life-discipline — of sleeping, eating, and work — but without actually taking up an Eastern technique as well. They report improvement in their lives as much as those in Eastern disciplines, and they seem equally unlikely to return to heavy drug use. In the same vein, I have known closely a number of practitioners of Eastern disciplines, some very experienced, who simply did not impress me as wiser or more evolved than they would have been otherwise. But in my research I have also brushed close to a tiny handful of individuals, some Oriental by birth, some Occidental, some young, most old, some male, some female, who radiated a certain quality, something almost palpable, whenever I was in their presence, something indefinable yet unmistakable: solidity, perhaps, or maybe wisdom, maybe love, but whatever its identity, more immediately convincing than any controlled study. I am not sure that every man or woman on the street could automatically reach that state merely by rigorously following a given Eastern technique (as some of the disciplines claim). Nor do I believe that Eastern techniques are the unique route to it: I have known two Westerners whom I think had little contact with the East, one a world-famous scientist, one a little-known old man, who unequivocally *had* that quality, too. Even more striking to me was that both of them so closely resembled their Eastern counterparts. However one gets there, it seems, the end state is remarkably the same; it is something very definite, very real.

We have strayed far from the original issues of fakery and self-discipline, but perhaps it has been of value to the reader. Spared some of the guesswork about my biases and beliefs in this area, he or she will now be in a better position to assess how much those beliefs have tinged my conclusions.

To return then: this chapter and the previous one have together dealt largely with meditators' most concrete, physical reasons for starting on the road East, particularly with their reaction to technology. Their view of the technological environment, as we have seen, reduces to two central beliefs: that it is *toxic* and that it is *fake*. And although many Americans share such feelings to at least some extent, the meditators are strikingly more sensitive to the toxicity and the fakery than other people, enough so that they have felt obliged to alter their lifestyles in response.

Why are they more sensitive? We have advanced one general reason for this, namely that meditators have had an unusual degree of exposure to technology, a maximal chance to witness it at its worst as well as its best. First, as members of the more affluent half of the world's most affluent society, they grew up surrounded by technological sophistication, and therefore in the midst of materialism, complexity, and artificiality. Secondly, their youth has coincided with a period of increased national awareness of poison and pollution, of strong statements for consumer protection, and of increased commentary on the less tangible dangers of the scientific worldview. Being well educated and acquainted with such dangers, they have joined in that awareness and contributed to it. Finally, and perhaps most importantly, almost all meditators spent a period of their lives in the drug culture. There they immersed themselves in material delights, saturated their desires for instant gratification, yet at the same time experienced poison and other dangers, and found transience and falsehood in artificial pleasures. The drug culture, in a sense, was an analogy of the larger society, but an extreme case in that it exposed youths at once to the most spectacular, the most sensuous, and also the most toxic, the most saccharine, that modern science had to offer. The drug scene was the *reductio ad absurdum* of technology.

Had these youths not experienced so intimately the technological milieu throughout their development, nor flirted so passionately with it in the drug world, perhaps they would not have "burned out" so quickly, nor swung so far to the opposite extreme of beliefs afterwards. Their lives constituted an accelerated course in the liabilities of technology; they graduated early with a certain insight, and a certain fear, that others would take much longer to acquire. In response, they turned to the East — as a retreat, a protection, and a discipline on which to base a new lifestyle.

5/ ANXIETY, ADULTHOOD, OLD AGE, AND DEATH

FRED

Fred Leonard lived down the corridor from me in my college dormitory in 1969. I best remember him in his most frequent pose in those days: playing poker. The door to his room was always open; periodically, clouds of cigarette smoke billowed out into the hall. In the hazy interior, Fred would be sitting at the card table with his friends, barefoot, wearing faded bluejeans and no shirt, usually with several days' beard on his lean face, and a perennial cigarette stub in his mouth. He did not remove the cigarette even to talk — the mark of an accomplished smoker.

He once described to me his daily routine in that year:

"It gets to be a regular thing. Sleep until about one o'clock in the afternoon, then hustle out of bed to make lunch before the dining hall closes. Then you come back to your room and fuck around for a few hours. Maybe even attend a class if you feel inclined. Then it's time for dinner. And after dinner it's only a couple of hours until it's time for the evening poker game. So you drink a little beer, smoke some dope, start playing poker around eight or nine, play until four or five in the morning, and then it's time to sleep again. So it goes on and on."

Only the advent of examination period broke the routine. Then, like many other students, Fred went into hibernation in his room, subsisting entirely on amphetamines and cigarettes, and learned the entire semester's worth of course material in ten days. He learned fast and usually managed to achieve reasonable grades by this method, although once he overdid the amphetamines and wrote a slightly psychotic final essay for a history exam.

I knew Fred only as an acquaintance in those days. As I recall, he finished his junior year in acceptable academic standing, then abruptly decided to take a year off. He went to Los Angeles for a couple of months, supporting himself with the previous year's poker winnings, and got into some fairly heavy drug use. He took LSD many times, had a couple of bad trips, and eventually left the city with a girl to tour the Northwest. Then he returned to New York and lived alone for the rest of the year in an apartment only ten blocks from his father's home. Apparently he did nothing in particular there, except to learn to play flamenco guitar. The next September he returned to college with much the same attitude as a year before. He quickly readopted the lifestyle of his junior year, minus some of the poker games, because he was so good that few dared play with him.

Toward the end of the first semester, he went through a period of heavy drinking and toyed with dropping out again, but finally decided to stick out the last few months. During May, in a rare flash of enthusiasm, he wrote a brilliant paper on the psychology of rock music for one course, in which he received an A. In the other courses he managed two Cs and a D by studying for a few days before the final exams.

I did not see him for many months. Then, on a rainy afternoon in November 1972, looking wet and weatherbeaten, he walked into the Cambridge center of the Students' International Meditation Society. Beneath his soaking brown coat, he was wearing baggy blue overalls with straps coming over his shoulders, a blue shirt, and heavy leather work shoes caked with mud. But though bedraggled he was fresh and alert, and as he smiled at me, he seemed more awake than I had ever remembered seeing him.

"Hey, I didn't know you'd taken up meditation," I said. "How long have you been doing it?"

"About a year. Barry turned me on to it. I was just coming here for checking this afternoon. I'm up in Boston for the weekend."

"Where are you living now?"

"In Harwich, down on Cape Cod. I live in a house there

with a bunch of four other guys and a girl. Three of them
are meditators. Harold is one of them — you remember him.
I spend most of my time down there now and come up to
Boston one or two times a month to see people. I came up
this weekend for a concert in the Garden."

"What are you doing on the Cape?"

"Three of us are working as carpenters. There's a lot of
summer-cottage building going on down there. It's enough
to employ a lot of people all winter, so we work pretty
steadily."

"That's interesting. I've met a lot of college guys who are
doing that kind of thing."

"Good men have started out as carpenters!" he said. "You
want to come down sometime?"

"Sure, I'll give you a ride back this Sunday."

Late Sunday afternoon we turned into the dirt road that led to his
house. We drove through half a mile of Cape Cod scrub-oak forest,
passed a shack with two rusted car bodies outside, and soon entered
a large cleared area, on the far side of which stood an old white Cape
farmhouse. As we drove up to the door, two muscular young dogs
bounded up to the car and barked in the windows.

The house was filled with the aroma of rice. Fred's roommates, Ellen
and Bob, were cutting up vegetables on a counter in the kitchen amid
bags of grain, small colored tins of tea, loaves of homemade bread, a huge
jug of honey, and a jar of big crystals of sea salt.

"We aren't really into that much of a heavy macrobiotic
thing," Fred said, as I peered around the kitchen, "but now
I'm eating a lot more grain, more fresh vegetables, and very
little red meat. I feel a lot healthier and also less aggressive."

"Less aggressive?"

"Yes. I've found that eating red meat definitely makes
me more mean and aggressive. I did an experiment: I stopped eating meat, then started eating it again. My level of
aggression fell when I stopped, and rose when I started eating it again."

"You really think that's true?"

"Yeah, like when a steer is about to be slaughtered, it
must experience a great deal of fear, so it wants to attack

whoever is about to kill it, right? So it suddenly has a great deal of adrenaline and maybe lots of other substances secreted into its bloodstream. Right? So when you eat the meat, you're eating those substances. Maybe that's the reason that it produces aggression."

"Well, it couldn't be adrenaline, because that would be destroyed when you digested the beef."

"Well, maybe it's not the adrenaline," he said. "I don't know exactly what it is. Probably it's some other substance."

It was nearly time for dinner. I wandered into the bathroom to wash my hands, and glanced into the medicine chest. No amphetamines, no sedatives, but an amazing array of vitamin preparations: multivitamins prepared exclusively from natural sources, B-complex vitamins, ascorbic acid in 500-milligram tablets, mixed tocopherols concentrate, calcium pantothenate, rose hips extract, biotin supplement, and two or three others, nearly empty.

Fred, Harold, Bob, and I meditated for twenty minutes, then joined the others for dinner. Conversation was quiet and slow, almost uncomfortably quiet, I felt. But then I was accustomed to the city. No one asked Fred or me about Boston; the talk covered food, music, the storm last week which had destroyed several beach houses on the Sound. At first there was little that I could contribute to the conversation, but at one point the subject got around to dishonest advertising. I mentioned some medically misleading advertisements for painkillers that I had recently seen on television. Everyone seemed interested; Bob asked me if one compound really produced kidney damage, and Harold wanted to know whether or not calcium was important to prevent digestive disorders. As I spoke to them the same vague sense of discomfort returned. I felt that I was talking too fast, perhaps a bit loudly, relative to the others. My style of conversation, which would have been perfectly natural talking with Fred and Harold in the dormitory two years ago, here seemed inappropriate; I had to make an effort to reduce myself to their level of quietness, of passivity. Too much red meat in my diet, perhaps.

After dinner Fred sat down with his guitar, his fingers almost automatically picking out a series of rasgueados, played slowly at first, then gradually faster, followed by a falsetta which I had heard him play before. He began to concentrate on his fingerwork, skillfully varying the falsetta, playing louder and faster as he grew more confident, until the room resounded with the savage, earthy impetuosity of Flamenco. A joint appeared from somewhere and circulated around the group, and we sat talking and watching him play in the candlelight. As the hours passed, the others, stoned and sleepy, went to bed, leaving Fred and me alone. He went to the kitchen and poured us each a large glass of wine.

"How did you come to be living here in the country and doing carpentry work?" I asked. "Was medi˙ ˙ ɔn a cause of it?"

"No, not exactly. Meditation was more an effect of it, if you see what I mean, in the sense that I came into contact with a lot of people who meditated, and eventually I decided to take it up myself. The way I got here — to Harwich — is that I knew Bob, and Bob told me that there were lots of openings for carpenters down here with pretty good pay. I've always sort of liked carpentry work, and it seemed like a good way to get out of the city."

"Why did you want to come down here rather than live in the city?"

"Oh, living in Boston just started getting to me. It was doing bad things for my head. You know, the pace of it, the whole atmosphere. I didn't even realize how much stress I was under until I came down and started living here. It was like a whole weight of anxiety was lifted off my shoulders. You don't realize how much of that anxiety there is, because you're accustomed to living with it in the city scene. But you ought to try coming down here and just living for awhile. You'd be amazed at the difference after being here for a month or two."

"Has meditation done good things for you?"

"Well, it hasn't exactly transformed my life or anything. But I didn't really believe it was going to do that, anyway. But there's been quite a difference. Before, the attacks of anxiety would really just throw me up against the wall. Now I still get attacks now and then, but they don't completely knock me over the way they used to."

"Attacks of anxiety? It was that bad?"

"Oh, Christ, man, it sure was. Starting around my last year in college. I used to feel the anxiety, sitting in the pit of my stomach, almost every morning when I woke up, and then during the day sometime I got attacks of it where I just stayed in my room for hours and felt too uptight to do anything at all. It really used to throw me right against the wall. I started drinking a lot, then, too. The anxiety didn't really begin to go away until I finally decided to move out of the city. And also the meditation, of course."

Fred's story has elements similar to other stories that we have heard before. The same dramatic shift of lifestyle, the same rejection of poison and artificiality are here. But why, as a Harvard graduate, is he working as a carpenter? Why his revulsion for the pace and stress of the city? What of his emphasis on avoiding aggression, or the whole air of almost enforced passivity that seems to hang over his group? Most of all, what is the meaning of his dramatic attacks of anxiety? How prevalent is anxiety among youths in Eastern disciplines, and what is its source?

The anxiety is amazingly prevalent, far more than I would have guessed before I first began talking deeply with individual youths. Few of them recognized its prevalence, either; many assumed that it was only themselves who were suffering from such anxiety, that they must surely have some personal psychiatric problems more severe than those of other people. They were astonished, and often relieved, when I informed them that I had heard nearly identical accounts from so many of their contemporaries. In fact, I am now convinced that only a minority of meditators over twenty-one have not experienced at least some period of major anxiety at some point in their development.

The anxiety has several origins. The first and most direct, once again, is from prior drug use. As youths emerged from the drug world with increased fears of poison and artificiality, so they also acquired a less obvious burden of anxiety. The anxiety was already beginning to become visible among some drug users when I wrote *Voices from the Drug Culture* in 1970 (see pp. 113-116): they had lost their wild, free, searching quality after two or three years of marijuana or hallucinogen use; their new desire was just to relax, to be comfortable and sedated. The search for sedation has reached far greater proportions. Listen, for example, to the following account from a yoga practitioner in New Hampshire:

"It's incredible now how many people are into alcohol. Everybody went through the same thing, of getting into grass and acid and then after a few years deciding that good old alcohol was the best thing after all. I almost never smoke grass anymore, but I drink all the time."

"But why is everybody doing alcohol now?"

"I don't know. People getting older, maybe. And more scared, sort of."

"But why more scared?"

"Well, less money around, fewer jobs around, maybe. The whole scene just isn't like it was five years ago, either. It just doesn't feel as good as it did. It doesn't have the excitement that it had, it's tighter, sort of. It just *feels* more uptight than it did in the old drug scene, if you see what I mean."

Others had more concrete experiences to trigger the anxiety, as in the account of a former big drug dealer named Clark:

"In the old days the whole scene was really beautiful, and I felt happy most of the time. And I felt important, too, because I was the biggest dealer in town. At least once a month I used to fly out to Arizona where I had my contact who got me grass from Mexico. Or just fly out there for a two-day vacation, because I was so rich from dealing that a couple of hundred dollars just didn't matter. It was a really groovy scene then. I could go to the library and pick up some girl there and take her home for the night, and there were always parties going on all the time, and incredible amounts of grass and acid, about half of which came through me. I was really confident then, and rich, too. People all looked up to me.

"The turning point came that time we got busted in New Hampshire. We didn't even have very much on us, just about ten caps of what I thought was LSD. Anyhow, this cop pulled us over for speeding, and somehow one of us had left a cap where it was visible on the dashboard. So the cop saw that, and then he searched the car and found the box with the others. I was standing there while he continued to look around, and I grabbed the box and threw it into the woods as far as I could. Of course then the cop got real mad, and one of them wrestled me to the hood of the car and then they put handcuffs on both of us. One of them stood guard over us while the other went and looked in the woods. It took him two and a half hours while we sat in the car, but he found the box, finally."

"That must have been pretty bad."

"Jesus, man, it was really hell, sitting in that car, not talking for two hours, and knowing that he wasn't going to give up until he found it. It was probably the heaviest scene that ever happened to me."

"So what happened?"

He laughed. "Well, you know what?" They sent the caps to the lab, and the stuff turned out to be MDA instead of LSD. And of course MDA was so new that the state of New Hampshire had never even heard of it and there was no law on the books saying it was illegal. So there was no way the pigs could prosecute us and we got off!"

"You could probably have even insisted that they return the caps to you!"

"Listen, man, I wasn't about to insist on anything then. The whole thing had just freaked me out too much. And my parents found out about it too, through the dean at the college, and that was a really heavy scene. You can't imagine what something like that is like unless you've been through it — the cops, judge, going to court, lawyers, the dean, getting suspended from college, and then the heavy scene with my old man after that. You'll never know what it's like. For two months afterwards I had to take Miltowns so that I could sleep, and sometimes I woke up in the middle of the night in spite of the Miltown, just shaking with fear. And it hasn't gone away yet. I don't dream about it anymore, or not very often, but I just don't feel the same confidence as I did in the old days."

A few months after this conversation, Clark took up a well-known Indian discipline. He instantly became very enthusiastic about it and within a matter of months it had become his entire life. He rapidly rose in the ranks of the organization, attaining higher levels of technique at the earliest possible time. Now he is one of three personal aides of an Indian master who has visited this country several times and who has an increasing following both here and abroad. When I last saw Clark, a few months ago, he was about to leave for India for the third time. We talked for an hour, and I found him even more devoted to the technique than before; in fact I could not get him to talk about anything else. It was hard even to imagine him as he had been in the old days. The anxiety is gone, too; now he radiates calm. Someday perhaps he will reach enlightenment through his technique, and I think someday he will become a great teacher.

Another friend named Joe, also a former heavy drug user and now a follower of Guru Maharaj Ji, managed to avoid frightening encounters with the law during his former days, but instead recalls an increased fear of crime in the drug world:

> "I'll tell you why there's more anxiety, as you put it.
> It's because the whole drug scene is a lot scarier than it used
> to be. Everybody gets ripped off, and kids get mugged on
> the streets and get their stuff stolen from them. The whole
> street scene has become a hairy place for a young kid to live.
> So what's happened is that the whole drug scene just doesn't
> feel comfortable anymore. It's gotten too heavy. The gentle
> days are gone, man."

Admittedly, the drug scene has always involved some degree of anxiety, in the sense that it has acted for many male youths as a test of toughness, of masculinity. But as Joe observed, it is much tougher now than before. This accounts for some of the increased "uptightness." And worse, it has lost the redeeming feature of *esprit de corps.* And in a more uptight atmosphere, it is little wonder that the "downs" — sedatives, narcotics, alcohol — should seem more attractive. What is the big-time drug right now in high schools and colleges? Methaqualone — Quaalude or "soapers" as it is often called — a drug which offers a lovely, smooth sedative effect, better than the barbiturates, more pleasing, to some than heroin.

The decay of the drug culture and the milieu of increased anxiety that it has created certainly have generated part of the anxiety described by meditators. But this fails to explain it entirely. For instance, there are a few meditators who have never used drugs, and some of them describe episodes of severe anxiety, too. What else is happening?

THE FUN'S OVER

We have come to a key issue. Let me introduce one more meditator,

Steve, a close friend and a student at Stanford Medical School. He is
now doing Ananda Marga, a technique similar to Transcendental Meditation, though less well known:

    "I went through an absolutely horrible period of anxi-
ety in my first year of medical school. In fact, I guess it
began in my senior year in college, about the time that I
had to make up my mind about what I was going to do after
college. Go to graduate school in biology? And get drafted
and sent to Vietnam? No. Go to Canada or something? Too
difficult. Go to divinity school? I almost did that, because
it was far-out and would have blown everybody's minds, but
I didn't. So I went to medical school.

    "As the time for starting medical school approached, I
found myself getting strange interludes of anxiety — just raw
fear, which would descend out of the blue when I was sitting
in my apartment or walking down the street. And the thing
that was really frightening about it was that it had no *cause*.
I wasn't anxious *about* anything. Medical school didn't scare
me. There was nothing specific in the near future that I had
to worry about. The flashes of anxiety just appeared randomly, unconnected to any actual fear-producing event.
That was what bothered me so much.

    "The thing reached its peak in the winter of my first year,
when I would have episodes lasting for hours two or three
times a day. I found my mind inventing theories to explain
the anxiety, like maybe I was being slowly poisoned by the
lead paint in my house, or I was having some rare organic
syndrome that produced these flashes of fear. And I developed rituals, too, to cope with it. I decided that if I drank
coffee out of one of my green-colored cups in the morning
instead of one of the white cups, I was less likely to get an
anxiety attack during the day. So I religiously drank coffee
exclusively from the green cups for months afterwards. It
seemed so strange, because I'm normally so scientific and
rational and all that, to see myself doing all these magic,
ritualistic things to get rid of the anxiety."

    "Knowing you now, it's strange to think of you believ-
ing in something like that!"

"Yeah, I know. And another strange thing that used to go through my mind. I had a funny feeling that I was growing old or nearing the end of my life, even though I was only twenty-one. I had a half-serious belief that my mind had some kind of ESP and could see into the future, and that it knew that I was going to die like maybe in a car crash six months later, and that it was feeling anxiety about the event in advance. Sort of a psychic phenomenon, in other words, my mind trying to forewarn me of my own doom. The whole thing was just another attempt to pin some kind of explanation on the anxiety, because if it was explained, it wouldn't be as frightening."

"Maybe your thoughts about dying had something to do with the fact that you were studying medicine."

"Maybe, but even several months before I actually started studying at medical school, I already had thoughts that maybe my health was going downhill. Those thoughts came in association with the anxiety. Sometimes I went to the gym and worked out just to demonstrate to myself that I was still in the same physical shape. Sometimes that helped the anxiety."

"And it was the year you started medical school that you took up Ananda Marga, wasn't it?"

"Yes. And the anxiety was one of the main reasons why. I felt desperate, and I wanted something, anything, to hang onto. So even though I wasn't sure that Ananda Marga would work, I did it faithfully. And it has worked. The anxiety has almost vanished. I almost never get it anymore."

The anxiety described by Steve sounds much like that in Fred's story, and I could supply a number of other stories like them. Both Fred and Steve place the onset of the anxiety in their last year of college, both had difficulty attaching an explanation to it or coping with it, and both cite it as a major reason for starting meditation. Both, curiously enough, use the actual word, "anxiety" — a rather technical word — in their accounts, rather than simpler terms like "fear" or "feeling scared." I think because it was the best word that they could think of to convey the abstract, free-floating quality of what they felt, the fact that it was not correlated with immediate events in their day-to-day lives.

An issue as diffuse as free-floating anxiety prompts one to invoke depth psychology, to try to offer some psychodynamic formula to account for it. For instance, is there any clue to the origin of Fred's anxiety attacks in the way that he has sublimated aggression or the fact that he chose to live so close to his parents during his year off? Did he perhaps perceive graduation from college, in fantasy, as entering into fearful competition with his father? Or in Steve's case, did the dim anticipation of dissecting cadavers in the anatomy lab, or having to treat dying patients, rekindle some anxieties from his own childhood? Such hypotheses are attractive; one can concoct them for every case. But although partially true, they seem too elaborate to be quite believable. Conversely, one can adopt simplified explanations, glibly attribute the anxiety to an "identity crisis" for example, but this is equally unsatisfying.

After hearing meditators recount their passage through a period of free-floating anxiety, I am convinced that the real common denominator of their experience was this: the anxiety appeared at the time that they perceived themselves at an interface between youth and adulthood. Rather than experiencing a smooth transition between the two stages — a satisfying, gradual increase in independence, responsibility, authority — they perceived instead a frightening gulf that must be crossed in a single bound, with little reward on the far side. Beneath the anxiety, in most of their accounts, was a shared sensation that something comfortable and safe was being irrevocably lost, and that something joyless and frightening would take its place. In simpler terms, "The fun's over. Now it's time to pay for it."

This is not new. Since time immemorial, adolescents have surely felt some anxiety about growing up. But many of the meditators became *profoundly* anxious; they felt a profound loss of the fun and were profoundly apprehensive about what they might have to pay. I offer this as an empirical observation, based on the material in numerous accounts, rather than as sociological theory, but I can suggest a number of theoretical reasons why it should be true. Quite simply, it appears that adolescence has never been so pleasant, adulthood so uninviting, or the emotional transition between them so unceremoniously abrupt, as in the lives of many of the meditators.

Consider Fred and Steve. Both first experienced their anxiety at the end of a long and comfortable existence in college. With their parents paying tuition, and no worries beyond occasional papers and exams, both were happy. There were no decisions to be made, no lifelong commitments to face. Of course, they were theoretically supposed to be planning for their potential careers. But coming from affluent homes, in affluent times, and attending liberal arts colleges, they felt no acute sense that they were preparing to earn a living. And so they postponed; they examined and criticized American society from afar, indeed learned new criticisms of it in their college courses, but postponed consideration of the fact that they themselves would soon be rather firmly asked to join it. Fred postponed even more concretely by taking a year off.

In addition, both spent much of their time in a largely recreational drug subculture. Smoking marijuana or tripping on LSD in the comfortable, relatively police-free environment of the campus, they were further detached from adulthood. In a hedonistic atmosphere, listening to sarcastic commentaries on the workaday world from such groups as the Mothers of Invention and the Rolling Stones, reading criticisms of the Establishment in underground newspapers and other literature of the drug scene, and reinforcing their beliefs in conversations with drug-using friends, they became even less enamored with orthodox careers.

And as time ran out and the end of college approached, the recreation ended. They quickly found themselves faced with a set of uniformly unpalatable alternatives: go to Vietnam, emigrate to Canada, get a draft deferment, take a job, or somehow, postpone further. Steve, being a straight-A student at Stanford, knew that he could easily get into medical school, thereby temporarily avoiding the draft. But his deeper reasons are revealing:

> "Well, I chose to go to medical school because it was the least of various evils. All the other alternatives were worse. And also, medical school put off the Real World, with a capital "R" and a capital "W," for another four years before I'd have to make further decisions. I guess in the back of my mind I hoped that I could create an extension of college by going to medical school, another four years where I really wouldn't have to work much and where I could stop and think what I wanted to do. But that didn't work, of course; I found myself in a world where I actually had to perform more, be evaluated. The Real World was too close."

Fred's situation was different; he had asthma and thus had no problems with the draft. But for him, too, the official alternatives upon graduation from college were intolerable. I remember that he once said: "You know, after you've been in a scene like in college, and done drugs, and played poker until five o'clock every morning, and generally had a ball, you can't go back to become a robot in the American machine. It would be *stupid* to go back. You *have* to find something else."

The majority of meditators between the ages of twenty-one and thirty had the same experience as Fred and Steve; practically all of them came from a socioeconomic class where they were expected to go to college, and most did. Also as a result of a background of affluence, few worked to pay their way in college and few spent time worrying about what work they would have to do afterwards. As for the academic workload, if it bothered Fred and Steve so little at Harvard and Stanford, it was even less an issue for most meditators at their institutions. They had even more time to devote to pleasure, especially drug use. College was a utopian interlude, magnificently isolated from the stifling conformism of workaday America.

Many, like Fred, took a year off, or even two, to postpone their confrontation with that conformism. For some, the year off merely perpetuated the utopia; for others, it represented a sincere attempt to get a preview of the outside world, to acquire some practice before the major confrontation was at hand. But most avoided a psychologically meaningful confrontation, denied the reality of what they would have to face, even when it became imminent. Hence, the nonspecific nature of the anxiety when it appeared; they still could not name what they were facing.

In passing, we should consider the objection that college has always been divorced from the real world to some extent. There is some truth in this. But it would be difficult to argue that there existed so large a gulf between college and adulthood during the Depression, during the War, even during the fifties. The events of the real world were much closer then. And there was markedly less affluence. Fewer youths went to college, and those who did considered college education a more serious thing. There was little to compare with the modern drug culture. A much smaller fraction of college students dropped out of college for a year or two, and far fewer left college permanently. In the last decade, what Erik Erikson has aptly called the "adolescent moratorium" has become more universal, more pleasant, longer, and more deeply divorced from adulthood than ever before.

Of course, the interface point, the anxiety point, does not always occur at the end of college. A few meditators experienced it near the end of high school; others, such as Clark, had it unexpectedly thrust upon them by outside circumstances. Many of the meditators younger than twenty have not yet reached it. Most important, a substantial number of meditators have ducked the anxiety entirely by simply refusing to acquiesce to the standard requirements of coming of age in our society. Instead, they have permanently dropped out of school or college, joined communes, started farming, journeyed to India, and tried scores of other unconventional alternatives to the sober official definition of adulthood. There is, naturally, a mixture of courage and cowardice in their decision — more of the former, I think, after talking to many of them — but unfortunately the Establishment and their parents recognize primarily the latter, and call it "copping out." As a result, though these youths have succeeded in bypassing the interface-anxiety, many instead pay in the coin of guilt, a problem examined in the next chapter.

Jim Mayer, for example, dropped out of college more than two years ago to move to his commune near San Antonio. His departure, by the way, had no relation to the "Contac" incident, which had occurred more than a year earlier and fortunately never reached the eyes of his parents or the dean. His avowed reason for dropping out is simple:

"I couldn't think of anything I wanted to do with my
degree, so why bother to get the degree? So I left. I can
go back if I want. I'm in good academic standing and all
that, and I would have to do three more semesters. Maybe
I will go back someday, just for the hell of it. But right
now, I feel really good where I am. I have no reason to go
back."

Jim has not experienced a period of severe anxiety. But perhaps he instinctively senses that he would if he went on to graduate. A degree, perhaps, would symbolize that more was expected of him; the pressure would be greater to take up a competitive position in a stressful society. But he emphatically does not want that, and so, in his words, why bother? In fact, he was even dissatisfied with the ambient anxiety of a low-key job in San Antonio. Listen to the degree to which "stress" — a frequent word in the doctrine of Transcendental Meditation — permeates his description of working in the city:

"I started off working for this small advertising firm.
They did a lot of radio ads and I worked doing a lot of the

electronic stuff for them — making tapes and doing mixing and editing, and all kinds of stuff like that. But there was something about the business — maybe it's the whole advertising business or maybe just that place which I didn't like. Because the people didn't really get along with each other. There was all this stress, sort of a negative energy in the air at the place. And if you worked there for awhile, it got into you. I could still feel the stress being carried along inside me as I drove back home from San Antonio at night.

"It was sort of a seductive kind of stress, though, if you see what I mean — you could get wrapped up in it, and if you did it for long enough, you probably would get to the point where you didn't even realize the stress was there. A lot of people live their lives like that, you know? I think that having done meditation has made me more aware of the presence of stress, like I sense it more quickly now when it's there.

"Anyways, I got out of the advertising place about six months ago, and now I'm working with this guy doing repairs on radios and TV sets. He's a very honest guy — doesn't try to rip off his customers — and I like him. I think I'll be able to get him to start meditating, too. We've talked about it a lot now.

"So I feel pretty satisfied. But what I'd really like to do would be to live in a commune and to farm. I mean, we are living in a commune now, really, but I'd like to be able to make it self-sufficient so that none of us would have to subject himself to the stress of the city just to get money."

"What is it that is so bad about that stress of the city, though? I would think that now that you've been meditating, you'd be better able to cope with that stress, that it wouldn't get to you as much."

"Oh, yes, absolutely. My ability to handle it has gone 'way up. Particularly if something really stressful happens, like my car breaks down when I'm in the middle of nowhere driving along. Three years ago that sort of thing would have really hassled me, but now I can handle it and not let it

bother me too much. But still, the point is, why have to
deal with the stress at all? I think that it still slows down my
evolution; every time that I have to use some of my energy
to counteract some sort of stress, it slows down my progress toward cosmic consciousness."

A little farther along in the same conversation: "When I
get home from work and come into our house I can just
feel the difference. That always seems to be true when
there's a group of meditators living together in a place.
There's a positive energy that exists around it and inside
it. There's a sort of way in which a group of meditators re-
inforce each other, because you have all these positive vibrations reinforcing themselves, you know? There's no stress
in the atmosphere, no negative things. When I come back
into the house after having been in San Antonio for the day,
it's as if I was casting off all of the negative things that I
accumulated in my body and in my mind during the day."

One might, again, postulate personal psychiatric problems to account
for Jim's intolerance of stress, but this fails to explain why the same intolerance occurs on such a massive scale, among thousands of other youths
in Eastern disciplines. It seems more likely that having grown up amidst
unprecedented comfort and the relative absence of stress, they are simply reluctant to begin ingesting massive doses of it as professionals or
businessmen in the modern world.

HEALTH, OLD AGE, AND DYING

A second empirical observation also suggests that the fear of adulthood is uncommonly severe among meditators. This is the fact that at
the tender age of twenty or twenty-five, occasionally even in their teens,
they are peculiarly preoccupied with growing old, even with dying. Some
of this we have already seen reflected in their concern with health and
with poisoning. But more specific imagery of old age and dying also
regularly emerges in their accounts, often without probing. An example
is Steve's mention of working out at the gym to prove that he had not
deteriorated in physical shape, or Ellie's suggestion that after the teen
years, the body lost the resilience to withstand the onslaught of Fillmore

concerts. I also recall a very direct statement from Harold, one of Fred's roommates at Harwich, who proved to be the owner of most of the vitamins in the medicine chest:

"You know a funny thing, Skip, is that I'm beginning to feel myself getting old. Like I go to bed and my arthritis hurts."

"But you're being facetious, aren't you? You don't really have arthritis?"

"Well, no, I guess not. But I'm getting really conscious that my body just isn't quite as forgiving as it used to be. It seems to take me longer to get over colds, or to recover from hurting my foot. Things like that."

Possibly Harold has been more sickly recently, but I doubt it; working as a carpenter, he looks far healthier than he did studying for exams two years ago. Certainly his present regime of organic food and vitamins represents some improvement over his college diet of Coca-Cola and potato chips. And he is still only twenty-three years old.

But in another sense, twenty-three years marks the beginning of old age in our society. It ends a golden period of life, a period more highly worshipped in our culture than in any other. Harold is no hypochondriac; he merely feels himself slipping downhill from the golden era into an adulthood that in America is increasingly devalued. From his vantage point, adulthood — or at least an ordinary one — signifies lesser rather than greater freedom, narrowed rather than expanded opportunities for pleasure and happiness. And in our sex-appeal society, adulthood offers in return very little enhanced status; stiff joints are the only compensation. Little wonder, then, that Harold should migrate to an Eastern discipline with the reverse value-pattern, where older age represents greater prestige, increasing wisdom, and a richer kind of happiness.

One might at first think Harold's "arthritis" an isolated case, or Steve's talk of health and dying merely a classic symptom of "medical student's disease." But looking deeper into the thoughts of other meditators, the old-age and death themes appear again and again. Consider this conversation with a boy named Cliff, a Zen meditator living near New Haven. It began when I noticed a big bottle of vitamin E, 600 international units per capsule, on his bureau.

"Why do you take vitamin E?" I asked. "Doesn't it cost a lot of money?"

"Yes, it's more expensive than most. I suppose that, being trained in the medical establishment, you're going to tell me that it's worthless."

"Well, I don't really know. I don't know much about the research done on vitamin E," I hedged.

Sensing my skepticism, he replied, "Well, look at it this way. Vitamin E may be of no value at all. But what if it is? Even if there's only a very small chance that it is necessary, I don't want to take that risk." He smiled. "It's rather like the way a not-very-devout Catholic looks at Hell. Even if he's pretty sure that there really isn't such a thing as Hell, he can't be absolutely certain. There's always just a small chance that there really *is* fire and brimstone down there. So he decides to pray, just in case. Because if he didn't pray, and it turned out there *was* a Hell, it would be a real bummer!"

"Yeah, I see what you mean, that if it's your health that's involved, you don't want to play around, don't want to take even a small chance. But you didn't feel unhealthy *before* you started taking the vitamin E, did you?"

"No, I admit it, it probably hasn't made any difference. But I still have that feeling of not wanting to take the chance."

"So what you're saying is simply that health has become very important to you, yes? You have put a very high premium on it so that you don't feel comfortable fooling around even with small risks. Am I interpreting you right?"

"Yes, I guess so. But the other thing is that it's so easy to take vitamin E each morning. It's not as if I were going to some great effort to avoid that risk."

"But what does it cost?"

"Only about six cents a day."

"When I knew you two years ago, though, I cannot remember you ever talking about health. And now it has risen so much in importance. What has gone on in your mind that has made it so much more important?"

He considered the question for a long time, then continued: "I don't know. I see what you're asking, but it's hard to pinpoint what the feeling is. I guess I just don't feel as young as I used to, and I don't want to see my body gradually get unhealthy, the way that I have seen it happen to so many older people. It matters to me more, to stay in good health, and I think I will, even when I'm forty or fifty."

"Do you really think much about getting older, about actually being forty or fifty?"

"Yes, I do think about it. I must think about it a little every day. It really is on my mind quite a lot."

"Do you ever think about dying?"

"Occasionally, but then everybody does. Dying . . . . that reminds me of an interesting story. A Zen master was talking to his students and he said, 'Life and death are actually the same thing. The difference we perceive between them is an illusion.' So some brash young student got up and said, 'Well, if that's the case, why don't you just go out and kill yourself?' To which the master replied, 'But what would be the point? They're the same thing!' I don't know whether that story's really true or not, but maybe, if I do Zen for a few more years, I can transcend that illusion, too. Then I won't be scared of dying anymore."

I know Cliff well; he is not stupid or misinformed. He does not believe that vitamin E will create some magical transformation in his well-being. Nor is he rich. Yet he spends twenty dollars a year on that one vitamin alone, and at least another fifty dollars on others. At the age of twenty-one he is scared, scared of losing his health as though he were an old man. And there are thousands, probably hundreds of thousands, of youths like him. For most, of course, the issue of growing old or of death does not surface so easily in a short conversation. In many it is entirely unconscious, yet images of declining health and advancing years appear with undeniable regularity in their accounts. And here they are, in their teens or in their twenties, practicing techniques once reserved for white-bearded old hermits in Himalayan caves.

In short, the health and old-age anxieties, like the episodes of free-floating anxiety described earlier, signify the loss of youth — the fun time, the safe time, the culturally worshiped time — and the onset of greater worries and obnoxious demands for a scheduled, competitive existence. For some, the ritual use of vitamins, like Steve's little ritual with the green coffee cups, insulates against part of the anxiety. Some mitigate anxiety by the scrupulous avoidance of fantasied poison, artificiality, and complexity, which often serve as the outward projection of it. Others smother it pharmacologically with alcohol or methaqualone. But the East, by far, answers most perfectly to the anxiety by attacking it simultaneously on all fronts. As the different characters in this chapter in turn have illustrated, the road East can provide a welcome exit from the drug world, a gentler and more unified subculture, an alternative set of values to those of a conformist American lifestyle, a graceful compromise between a carefree youth and a workaday adulthood, and a philosophical rationale for retreating from stress and seeking a less demanding country life. Most significantly, nearly every discipline promises, and delivers, a very practical sort of psychotherapy, a personal reinforcement against anxiety. Techniques requiring daily exercises, such as meditation, yoga, or chanting, not only systematically teach relaxation, but as Fred or Steve asserted, may help to lessen anxiety as a whole. And to those youths who practice no actual technique, including, for instance, followers of Meher Baba and Guru Maharaj Ji, the mere fact of experiencing the love of the master may be more rewarding than any therapeutic system. Finally, unlike most Western psychotherapy, the East offers the hope of ultimately surmounting even the great, deep, existential anxieties of growing old and dying, a chance of attaining the equanimity of the cryptic old Zen master who said that life and death were the same thing. Though that blissful state shines at the distant end of the road, to be reached only be a few, it is an inviting glimmer to some youths for whom those existential anxieties are no longer deep at all.

Anxiety is probably the most important of the emotional stimuli which lead youths to adopt Eastern disciplines, but it is not the only one. The chapter that follows deals with an almost equally prominent emotional feature of meditators: guilt.

6/ GUILT, AGGRESSION, AND THE RIGHTEOUSNESS GAME

CORY

Cory Randall, in his college days, was a fairly heavy marijuana smoker and had used LSD about thirty times. He was also quite a drinker, particularly during the summer when he worked in Maine. He could put away two six-packs of beer on a heavy evening, sometimes even three. And starting at about the age of seventeen, he was something of a ladies' man, keeping track of the number of girls he had scored with, and even surreptitiously keeping an eye on the corresponding figures for his friends. To put it less delicately, he was a male chauvinist pig, a successful one, and he was proud of it. We were good friends in college and exchanged many stories about our lives. I quoted Cory on two occasions in *Voices from the Drug Culture* (pp. 33 and 39). Both accounts are worth repeating to give some idea of his thoughts in those days:

> "My father was a doctor. He saw the whole world through a microscope and listened to it through a stethoscope. I never had any real communication with him, and I don't think my mother had much either. I remember when I was in prep school and I made it with a girl for the first time, I told him about it in a letter, just to see if it would break through his shell. He wrote back and had the audacity to say that I was 'sick' for doing it. Sick! And then he never talked about it again. That's one of the few times I ever had any communication with him at all."

And, on a later occasion:

> "You know I've been going with another guy to a spade
> bar in Central Square. And it's so different from all of the
> people here. Those people live and love their way through
> every minute of life, Skip. A guy is measured there by the
> quickness of his repartees and his fists, and how much alco-
> hol he can hold, and whether or not he's ever shot up skag.
> I can't go on in this nice, quiet life in college until I've seen
> how I shape up in that world."

Shortly after the time of the latter conversation, Cory left college. He lived in an apartment in North Cambridge for awhile, then vanished. None of his friends knew where he had gone. Then, two years later, in late 1972, my telephone rang and a voice said, "Is Skip there?" "Speaking." "Bet you don't know who this is!" The voice was familiar but I could not place it. But when it broke into a deep, rolling laugh, I instantly knew it was Cory. He was no longer a playboy; he had been married for two years, and he had a son! I found it very hard to imagine Cory as a family man. He was working as a counselor in a drug rehabilitation center in a small town in western Massachusetts, again a surprise.

Another of his old friends, Jack, and I drove out to see him. When we arrived, he embraced each of us tenderly. Then I knew for certain that something in him had changed; three years ago, he would have re-garded such a gesture as verging on homosexuality.

We went to lunch at the bar next door. Neither he nor his wife or-dered meat; they had not been eating meat for nearly a year now, he said. But even more astonishing, he ordered a tall glass of quinine water and lime, minus the gin. No, he had not been drinking for a year, either. I even thought I saw a flash of disapproval in his eye as I ordered a beer.

> "Why did you stop eating meat?" I asked.

> "Well, Sue turned me on to it after we got married. She
> showed me a really interesting book, called *Diet for a Small
> Planet*, which shows how inefficient it is for you to live off
> the top of the food chain. Do you realize that a steer has to
> be fed twenty-one pounds of protein in the form of a grain
> to produce one pound for human consumption? After read-
> ing through that book, I began to realize how much I was
> wasting the earth's resources by eating meat."

> "That's quite a change from when I knew you before. You
> feel bad about the waste of that grain?"

"Well, yes, in a way, when you consider how many people
are starving and need food all over the world, and here we are
in America feeding all that precious food to *animals* so that
we can slaughter them and eat meat."

Our meals arrived at that point. Jack looked sheepishly at his hamburger then hesitantly began to eat it. The conversation continued. At
one point, Sue remarked,

"We grind our own flour at home, too."

"But is it any different from buying ordinary stone-ground
flour at an organic food store?" Jack asked.

"Oh, it's better, and fresher," Cory replied. "And it's part
of the whole thing of trying to get away from processed things.
Since you do none of the work producing them, processed
foods separate you from the earth, from a real appreciation
of what you're eating. One lazy gesture, and you eat it and
forget where the food came from."

I asked him about his new abstinence from alcohol.

"I guess I decided that since I was stopping using drugs
I should stop using alcohol, too. I was drinking more than
I should, anyway."

"Did it have anything to do with your starting to work
here at this drug rehabilitation place?"

"Yes, maybe. Having come out of drugs myself, I wanted to be able to go back and help other people with their
problems, to help them get out, too."

He spoke softly, so softly that I barely heard him above the din at the
bar. I suddenly noticed the same vaguely uncomfortable feeling that I
had at Fred's dinner table in Harwich a month earlier; the sense that I
was talking too loudly, being somehow too aggressive, in comparison
with him. Four years ago, the comparison would have been the other
way around.

After lunch, Jack and I talked to him alone in his counselor's office.

"What are you going to be doing in the next few years?"
Jack asked.

"Sue and I are going to work here one more year until we
have saved up a little more money. Then we're going to buy
some land, probably on Cape Breton Island in Nova Scotia,
and farm."

"Can you live by just farming?"

"Oh, yes, there's good land up there, and it's still cheap.
A lot of good people are moving out there, now, because it's
getting too expensive to buy a farm in Maine or Vermont
anymore."

"Why do you want to do that?"

He paused and thought for a second, "I guess, basically,
because I don't like to work hard. I won't want to lead the
sort of constant working life my father did, and I don't want
to do something in the city."

"But isn't it hard working on a farm?"

"That's what most people think. But you should pick up
a book called *Living the Good Life* by Helen and Scott Nearing. They've farmed for about forty years after they left
their jobs in New York City. And they got it so that all they
had to do was work only a half-day each day, and they always had time to do all the other things they wanted to do."

He went on talking ecstatically about his plans for buying a farm. Already he had made a trip to Nova Scotia to check out various possibilities. He had several close friends who had been successfully farming in
Maine for more than two years. Two of them, he said, did Transcendental Meditation. I asked him if he had considered doing meditation.

"No, I don't think I'm ready for meditation yet. I don't
think I've advanced quite to that point. But Sue and I went
to see a yoga teacher, a young woman in Northampton, and
we've been doing yoga now for several months. It's been
very good, and it's done good things for me. Maybe I'll go
on and try meditation, too."

Later in the conversation, he asked Jack, "What are your
plans?"

"Well, now that I've been accepted at medical school, I
think I'll go on and be a psychiatrist."

"A psychiatrist? That's interesting." Cory paused.
"Don't take this amiss, but you have never struck me as a
particularly *warm* person. I'm not saying that to be critical. I'm sure you know that. But do you think you'd make
a good psychiatrist?"

Jack was visibly taken aback for a moment. "Well, I'm

not sure that it's always necessary to be warm to be a good psychiatrist," he said, hesitantly.

"Yeah, maybe not."

We continued talking for awhile, took a tour of the center, and then decided that it was time to leave. Just before we left, I asked him, "What is it that has caused you to change to much during these years?"

He looked at me and chuckled warmly. "Skip, the psychologist, always sitting there with his mental notebook, asking probing questions!" He mused for a while. "I think it had something to do with my parents. I don't know. And also, maybe something to do with going to Sunday School when I was a kid, some sort of unconscious religious things from the past, maybe."

He embraced both of us again before we left.

As soon as Jack and I were together in the car on the way back, we looked at each other in amazement.

"You'd hardly know it was the same guy!" Jack said.

"Yes, the machismo thing he used to have has vanished. Now he has an air of guilt, and there was something about him that at times made me feel ill at ease. He seemed sort of —"

"Righteous?"

"Exactly!"

What happened to Cory? Where had the aggression gone, the quest for tough masculinity in his old account of the Central Square bar, or the anger that emerged in his story about his father? Could they have simply evaporated? And what of the guilt and the righteousness which have taken their place? Did the Puritan ethic catch up with him, unexpectedly?

Cory's metamorphosis is not uncommon; many people in Eastern disciplines convey the same vague sense of guilt, the same righteousness, the same qualities of somehow being almost *too* nice, *too* gentle, to be quite believable, particularly if one also had the opportunity to know them a few years before. It is important to clarify this, because guilt ranks with anxiety as one of the most frequent reasons for going East, although the mechanism involved is entirely different.

Some of the guilt stems from immediate sources — guilt about former hedonism in the drug world, or about having dropped out of college or otherwise having failed to conform to parental or societal expectations. Further guilt is added for those who decide, in the Establishment's words, to permanently "cop out"; to work as a farmer or a carpenter instead of in father's business or some other approved profession. In other words, as some youths experience a spike in their anxiety level at the youth-adulthood transition point, others seem to have a spike of guilt. It is usually unconscious guilt; Cory, of course, does not consciously believe that his new decisions are wrong. But the conscious recognition that he is right obviously does not prevent the emergence of the guilt.

In addition, as Cory acutely observed, the guilt may often come from the more distant past, from a religious background or (for males) Oedipal guilt stemming from the belief that one had mother's love at father's expense. The latter would be a logical outcome of the classic American family pattern of distant father and close mother. As we have suggested in an earlier chapter, many youths in all Eastern disciplines, like Cory, share such a background.

And the aggression? It is still there, but expressed in a subtle and curious way — by righteousness. In Cory's case, consider the implication that meat eaters are wasting earth's resources, the assertion that Jack was not a warm person, the "Skip the psychologist" remark, or the discomfort he unwittingly created in us at the bar. Of course such statements have a basis in truth: Meat *is* an inefficient source of protein, and here I am, playing psychologist. But nevertheless, Cory is using these statements to play a game, a game of the same form as those described by Eric Berne in *Games People Play.* We might call it the "righteousness game."

A naked prototype of the righteousness game is the "you are not a warm person" statement. This is an aggressive statement, really one of the more undermining things that one can say to another human being. But when White pronounces the statement *warmly* and covers it with, "I'm not being critical," Black has no good reply (aside from a metastatement of the form, "You are playing a game, you bastard"). If Black gets angry and cold, it only further proves White's original point. If Black says, "You have hurt me," White also looks hurt and counters, "But I explained that I was not being critical. Don't you appreciate that I'm just being your friend and trying to help?" The key to the game is that White has implicitly defined *himself* as a warm person, and, hiding behind that definition, is free to express his own anger and aggression as much as desired. The same analysis, with appropriate modifications, applies to many other situations, as for example, the case of some vegetarians (not *all* vegetarians) who disapprove of meat eaters with the implication that eating meat represents cruelty. An even simpler example is the popular "Warning — I brake for animals" bumper sticker, implying, insidiously, that ordinary drivers do not.

The beauty of the game, of course, is that it protects White from his own guilt by making somebody else feel guilty instead. If White has Black on the defensive with a statement like, "You are not warm," then White is temporarily spared from any gnawing doubts he may have about his own capacities for warmth. Analagously, one can imagine Cory saying to society (or, psychoanalytically speaking, his father), "You who are aggressive, meat-eating and alcohol-drinking, you lazy processed-food eaters, with your cold, empty, urban lives, how can you *possibly* feel justified in accusing *me* of copping out?" Of course, society is actually not justified, but unconsciously, he's afraid it is.

The righteousness game is as old as human communication; I fancy that the Puritans may have once created some animosity by playing it in old England. Perhaps it even had something to do with the fact that they were hustled out of Europe and founded America. It is a familiar game; we have all played White and Black at different times. But I have belabored the familiar for a good reason: the righteousness game is played so regularly by certain people in Eastern disciplines that they have alienated many otherwise neutral outsiders. For example, I think that a certain fraction of readers will instantly empathize with an older friend of mine:

> "Well, there's something I just can't stand about these meditator types, that just makes me mad. It's that they act sorry for you because you haven't seen the light, because you don't follow their latest guru, or because you eat meat or drink cocktails or smoke cigarettes. I've been with groups of them a couple of times, and I immediately got fed up.
>
> "I remember one of these times I asked some girl, 'What do you do when you do Zen?' She first put on a very calm, blissful expression and smiled condescendingly, and then replied in a very soft voice, 'Oh, Zen is not something that I can explain to you in words. It's only something that you can understand by doing.' Then I said, 'Well, sure, I know that it's a nonverbal thing and all that, but what do you ac-

tually *do*?' Then she looked at me as though I were talking
too loud, and said, even more softly, 'What you should do
if you have any serious interest in Zen is to go and spend a
period of time in a Zen community.'

"Her whole reaction was so fake that I lost any belief I
might have had in the whole thing."

But this is not real Zen at all. For whatever words there may be to
describe Zen, it is not fake. And this brings up the whole issue of the
misuse of Eastern disciplines.

SOME USES AND ABUSES OF THE EAST

Among meditators, probably the most common playing field for the
righteousness game is the axis of passivity and aggression. As an example, I am reminded of an occasion when I walked into an office room at
a meditation center in New York. As I entered, the girl behind the desk
looked up at me with a slightly angry, disapproving expression, then
looked down at my feet. It was quite clear from her gesture that my
shoes had been too loud. Yet no one was meditating nearby and she her-
self was also wearing shoes. She simply disapproved of my noise on general principle, it seemed, implying that a properly devout meditator in
her organization would not make noise like that. A permuted line from
"Wooden Ships" flashed across my mind; and I could almost hear her
saying, "I can see by your shoes my friend that you're from the other
side." At any rate, I was appropriately embarrassed and tiptoed there-
after.

But do Eastern disciplines actually require such a cult of gentleness
and passivity? It is definitely not a criterion for reaching enlightenment.
In fact, the enlightened man is anything but passive. He possesses great
calm, yes, and is free of *inappropriate* anger and aggression, but he is
capable of forceful energy, great activity, even violence. For example,
the great Zen master Nan-ch'uan (748-834) once encountered his disciples disputing the ownership of a cat in the monastery. Raising his
spade, he threatened to slice the creature in two unless one of them
could immediately express the essence of Zen. There was utter silence,
and — mash! — what would the "I Brake for Animals" people have said?
Think also of Judo, Japanese fencing, the Samurai — all spawned by Zen

— or of Lord Krishna and Arjuna on the battlefield in the Bhagavad-Gita,
or of Christ throwing the money changers out of the temple. These were
not soft men. Even the practice of meditation itself, whether it utilizes
a *koan*, as in Japan, the sound of breathing, in Tibet, or a mantra, in India, is distinctly not a passive activity; if it were, one would profit just
as well from falling asleep. The last thing that meditation aspires to do
is create a lukewarm, dishwater personality. It does not seem the fault
of the East, then, that some meditators assume a guise of righteous
passivity.

On the other hand, in defense of their approach, one can attribute
some of the meditator's passivity to the fact that aggression has become
increasingly unacceptable with advancing technology; one cannot be a
Samurai in the thermonuclear age. Only within the present generation,
we must recall, has it become possible for the aggression, selfishness, or
even accidental neglect of a few men to poison, impoverish, and anni-
hilate entire populations. It was a century ago that Nietzsche observed
that advancing civilization demands a difficult domestication of the old
instincts, and when the instincts, inevitably, persist in wanting gratification, guilt results. Now, more than ever, it can be argued, it is better to
be a little guilty than to tolerate the atrocities that can occur when aggression and other passions are unleashed. Considering what they have
seen while growing up in modern times, both in the media and closer
to home, meditators seem quite justified in valuing passivity and gentleness, even in excess.

This is a nice reason, but rarely the real reason. Instead, a number of
meditators, like the Zen girl in the quotation earlier, use passivity as a
way of covertly expressing anger, of demarcating their side from the
other side, as a way of saying, "I have no aggression and you have it
all." In addition, this serves other purposes: defense against anxiety
by implicitly segregating oneself within the subculture, and defense
against guilt via the righteousness game.

Another girl, a Transcendental Meditator named Sheila, once remarked:

> "Now that I've been meditating for two years, I find that
> there are some of my old friends that I just can't be around
> anymore, because they create too much stress around them-
> selves. They just create bad vibes when you're with them, you
> know? After you've been meditating for awhile, and your

own nervous system gradually gets rid of that sort of thing,
it gets so that you become very sensitive to it in other people. I went back to see two of my old friends in L.A. last
month, and I was really surprised. I found that I just couldn't
stand being with them anymore. They seemed so — so loud,
and they just created an uncomfortable atmosphere around
them."

"But they were your good friends before?"

"Yes."

"Have *they* changed, maybe? Become more stressed, perhaps?"

"No, I don't think so. The problem is that they haven't
changed because they haven't started meditating. Actually,
they don't even believe in meditation at all."

Now it is conceivable that meditation actually has purged Sheila's
own aggressive tendencies. But it seems at least equally plausible to suppose that she has simply projected all of her own aggression onto her
nonmeditating friends, and then, basking in her own dubious purity, has
proceeded to get righteously angry at them for their "bad vibes." Little
wonder they should not believe in meditation after such treatment.

There is a second significant way in which the righteousness game is
played by some youths on the road East. This is their tendency to in-
ject morality and asceticism into their disciplines far beyond the degree
actually required, to transform an innocent technique into an entire Cal-
vinistic religion. They seem to interpret "discipline" in the peculiarly
Western sense, as an atonement for guilt, something that has to hurt.
But the type of discipline required by the East is quite a different thing;
it is a mere tool to be used on the path to enlightenment. To use the
classic Zen analogy, it is like a boat that one uses to cross a body of water; once the far side is reached — success attained — the boat is left aside.

True, looking from the outside, it is sometimes difficult to tell
asceticism-as-repentance from asceticism-as-tool, but the distinction is
always present and has been clearly underlined by such writers as Fromm
and Watts. One distinguishing field-mark of the Western species — of
the guilty kind of morality and asceticism — is the tendency to regard
less moral and less ascetic outsiders as slightly inferior creatures. And a
certain small fraction of people in Eastern disciplines reek of this quality.

As just implied, righteous asceticism is almost never the fault of the

the Eastern disciplines themselves. Transcendental Meditation, for example, specifies no official requirements for diet, sexual activity, or behavior toward other people. Meher Baba, similarly, asks no sacrifices and no code of ethics, only that one learn to love him. And in Zen, if a rich man enters a monastery, he does not have to give away his possessions. In fact, to do so might reveal an undue concern for them; there is a subtle sort of pride, a faint scent of expressing one's superiority, in the act of giving them away. It is a false brand of asceticism and Zen has no use for that sort of thing. (One thinks of Nietzsche, again: though he attacks the East in the *Geneology of Morals*, he, too, recognized the "will to power" underneath that kind of "asceticism.") Likewise, one need not be a scholar of the East to realize that deliberately sleeping on a straw mat with a block of wood for a pillow will do nothing, *per se*, to accelerate one's progression to enlightenment. Even sexual abstinence, demanded by a few, and only a few, Eastern disciplines at certain levels, lacks the righteous quality often attached to it in Western religions.

These are but a few examples. For further discussion of asceticism and morality in the East, or rather, the absence of them in the form that Puritanism has taught us, the reader is referred to numerous works in the Reference Notes, especially those of Watts. The point here is that many youths are using Eastern disciplines as excuses for practicing a guilty and self-righteous brand of asceticism and morality. And when the smoke has cleared, their practice is serving the same old purpose: resurrecting childhood religious training, expressing repentance to parents and society for copping out, and more covertly, expressing anger at parental figures by barricading off the Eastern subculture and playing righteousness.

A common and simple case of this occurs among yoga novices who assume that the exercises must involve strain, or ideally, hurt if they are to do any good. Some seem almost disappointed when their teachers keep insisting that that is not the point at all. Fasting is another example. Some do it in the name of health, to "clean poisons out of the system"; others do it in genuine quest for enhanced spiritual vision. But about a third of the fasters that I have met, whatever philosophical rationale they gave for their practice, not only exuded guilt in their own personalities, but tirelessly sought to impose it on their more omnivorous friends. I have occasionally been tempted to suggest to them the alternative of flagellation; it is faster and does not deplete body stores of vitamins.

A more complex example of guilty asceticism emerges in the following conversation with a boy named Chuck at an ashram in Vermont. I am the second speaker.

"You do Transcendental Meditation? Well, that's nice, but it's not *really* an Eastern technique."

"Sure it is!"

"Well, I guess, in a way, but it's just twenty minutes morning and evening, isn't it? It's only sort of a psychological thing that makes you feel better from day to day. But otherwise you go on living your same life, don't you? All your other activities are unchanged, aren't they?"

"Well, that's not *entirely* true, but, basically, yes."

"Well, I'm not saying that TM is *bad* for you. In fact, it's probably a very good thing, a good preparation, but I don't think you can really get very far until you actually live in a commune for awhile and actually do it with your whole life! I mean, I'm not saying there's something wrong with your life now. It may just be your Karma at this time in this life to be a medical student, and that's good. Go on and finish being a medical student. But then, if your spiritual development really matters to you, you have to live the right kind of life for it."

He went on to describe life in his ashram: getting up at 5 a.m., meditating until seven, scheduled chores and exercises during the day, a formal group discussion in the evening, further hours of meditation before bed. It *was* a good life for spiritual development, no doubt about that, but what I objected to was the supercilious air with which he presented it.

"How is it that you first came here?" I inquired.

"Well, it was after I got out of high school that it all started. During that next year I had two or three experiences that really awakened me. They were sudden feelings of understanding, very hard to describe. I later learned that they were flashes of a high level of consciousness. That is what first taught me that there was something important there, waiting for me."

"But it was at least another year before you came here, yes?"

"Yes."

"What happened in the meantime?"

"I went to college for a few months, but I quickly realized that it was leading in the wrong direction, doing bad things for my Karma."

"I never knew you had spent those months in college. I guess I thought that you had decided in advance that college would be that way, and that you did not want to go."

"That's true. I really didn't want to go."

"They why did you go?"

"Well, I guess because my father pressured me to do it."

He was becoming justifiably irritated at all of my questions, so I stopped interrogating him. But he went on to mention that he had tried to convince his parents that they, too, should practice his particular discipline, although it was hopeless to persuade them to go to the extent of coming to an ashram. In fact, many of the others in his ashram had tried to convert their parents at one time or another. A few had succeeded, but Chuck's father, who happened to be a New York advertising consultant, would hear nothing of it, and apparently tried equally stubbornly to convert Chuck to coming back and living at home.

Now it is possible that Chuck actually is one of those exceptionally gifted individuals who, like Hui Neng, the Sixth Patriarch of Zen, experienced flashes of enlightenment before having ever received formal instruction. Yet Chuck did not strike me as possessing the genuine strength and understanding of some of the other members of his commune. Alternatively, a cynic might suggest that his "flashes" were brief psychotic episodes; that is possible, too. But the "flashes" seem to me less telling than the pride that he takes in the rigor and asceticism of his new lifestyle. Though the ashram regime is surely valuable in many ways, Chuck seems to be using it partially as a weapon against his father, as a way of saying, "See here, what I am doing is at least as rigorous and demanding as any work you wanted me to do. Not only that, but it is *better* than your work; you should convert to my side." Chuck has thereby effectively dealt with his guilt, but at some cost, I fear, to his potential spiritual development.

A simpler case, also with visible anger, comes from a Transcendental Meditator named Eric:

"I used to smoke cigarettes a lot, maybe two packs a day, and it did very bad things for me. It was all part of the type of life I lived then. I was eating bad food and sleeping badly, and it was all very negative. But almost right away after I started meditating I lost my desire for cigarettes, so I stopped and haven't had one since.

"Now it's gotten so that I can't even stand the smell of cigarette smoke, and I don't live anymore with people who smoke because it's bad for my meditation. One of my roommates at the Humboldt course smoked, and even when he had smoked in the morning and I came back to the room hours later in the afternoon, I could still smell the stink of cigarettes in the room."

"Did you do anything about it?"

"I tried to transfer to another room, but it was too late."

Again, it is possible that the reversal of Eric's cigarette habit was entirely the direct result of meditation, as he suggests. But it is hard to imagine that he could acquire such an exquisite distaste for cigarettes, or such an abhorrence of those who are smokers, without prior guilt about something in his own "negative" past.

Probably it is unnecessary to give further examples; many readers will doubtless think of others from their own experience. Or one can find them in a book such as *Be Here Now* by Baba Ram Dass, the former Dr. Richard Alpert. Though the book is a beautiful one, filled with genuine Eastern wisdom, one constantly encounters little outcroppings of the Puritan ethic in its pages. There is a difference, however: Ram Dass, unlike most of the other people quoted in this chapter, would be the first to admit that he retains some guilty morality from his former days; he rarely tries to play the righteousness game with it. Nor does he indulge in fake passivity; I can remember him after a lecture last year at Amherst, walking out serenely in his white robes, hopping into his sports car, and roaring off across the campus.

On the other hand, one can examine a work like the Nearings' *Living the Good Life* — one of the books cited by Cory — to find the righteousness game played in its most pristine purity. The book oozes guilt and morality both in its description of subsistence farming in Vermont and in its commentaries on modern American civilization. Throughout, the Nearings seem rather conspicuously satisfied with their own kindness and generosity. For example, though they are not *directly* referring to themselves, they explain that successful rural communes can be formed only by "The few, rarely endowed and supernormally equipped men and women who are willing and able to live as altruists after being trained, conditioned and coerced by an acquisitive, competitive, ego-centric social system" (p. 185).

But when they brand one individual as "number one man on Beelzebub's roster of real-estaters" (p. 8), condemn the laziness of eating processed food (p. 116), or decry the sloth and ineptitude of their next-door neighbors (pp. 152-153), the pages crackle with righteous anger. Nor do they sound entirely forgiving in the following:

> To the credit of Vermont conservation it must be said that during the two decades of our stay, after innumerable discussions and long-drawn-out arguments on the subject of white flour, white sugar, pies and pastries, the necessity for eating raw vegetables, and the revolting practice of consuming decaying animal carcasses, no native Vermont family of our acquaintance made any noticeable change in its food habits. (p. 159)

But though their righteousness may be obnoxious, the Nearings are good people, perceptive people, with much to say about evils in American society that anticipates the complaints of meditators twenty years later. The Nearings do not mention practicing an Eastern discipline themselves, but then *Living the Good Life* was written in 1954, when few techniques were available to learn in the United States. At any rate, the book graphically illustrates practically every theme so far described for the case of meditators, including "complexity, anxiety, waste ugliness, and uproar" (to quote them; p. 6), "slow poison in the human system" (p. 140), the preoccupation with health, and, of course, the idea of retreating from modern society to start a new program of life. Not surprisingly, the book is a bible for thousands of meditators, including many who do not abuse their disciplines in the ways described in this chapter.

•   •   •

I have stepped on toes, and I have risked losing some friends by writing this chapter. Both Sheila and Cory will doubtless recognize themselves when they see this book someday, and a much larger number of meditators will perhaps grudgingly concede that they too can recognize themselves, in a sense, saying some of the same things. A different group of readers, some of them opposed to meditation, and others, devout meditators themselves, will probably rise and applaud the fact that I was willing to denounce so bluntly the righteousness of that fraction of Eastern practitioners. But whatever animosities or alliances it generates, this chapter is necessary to disentangle the complex role that guilt plays for many youths on the road East. Although it frequently generates misinterpretations of Eastern philosophy, causes some to take up a particular technique for inappropriate reasons, and leads a few to play an obnoxious game, nevertheless guilt must be acknowledged as a major force in the decision to practice an Eastern discipline.

7/ SCIENCE, SANITY, MADNESS, AND MAGIC

The physical and emotional components in meditators' reaction to the Establishment, as we have seen, can indeed be far-searching and dramatic. But more immediately striking, and ultimately more profound, is their intellectual rejection of modern scientific thought, and even of the entire philosophical system on which it is founded. The more one listens to meditators, the more the magnitude of this rejection becomes apparent. For example, I vividly remember an argument that occurred in a small discussion group at a Transcendental Meditation course in California. The speakers, Jeff and Ken, are both college students from New England:

> "There's one thing that confuses me about this morning's lecture," Jeff began. "Maharishi starts by saying that it is the nature of life to evolve and to progress, and that everything in the universe is evolving and progressing on *all* levels. Now I can believe that things are evolving on *some* levels, but is it true on all levels? What about entropy, for example?"
>
> "What do you mean by entropy?" Ken asked.
>
> "I mean the fact that the universe is gradually slowing down. Everything in the universe is gradually going from a state of greater organization to a state of lesser organization, in other words. Eventually all the stars will burn out and the universe will be reduced to sort of a warm soup."
>
> "Well, how do you know that's true? I mean, what makes you sure that that's right?"
>
> "It's been proven scientifically. That's what the second law of thermodynamics is all about."

"That doesn't prove anything, just because physicists call it a law. I mean, how do you know that the universe is *really* slowing down?"

"Entropy has been demonstrated in hundreds of experiments, maybe thousands. Nobody has ever done an experiment which contradicted it."

"But that doesn't necessarily mean anything, just because somebody has done a bunch of experiments. How do you know that they're right?"

"But you don't understand. Entropy isn't just an abstraction or an idea. It's not just a theoretical construct. It's a *thing*. It's measurable. You can measure the entropy of a closed system. You can give it a number!"

"You don't expect me to believe in it just because you can put a number on it, do you?"

"Well, look at it this way. For entropy to be reversed would be like having a tube full of air, and having all the air molecules migrate to one end of the tube and leave a vacuum at the other. There's an infinitesimal chance that that could happen, according to the laws of probability, but the chances against it happening, even for a fraction of a second, are astronomical. What you're implying is that the whole universe could do something like that, permanently! That's impossible!"

"No, it's not impossible at all. Just because it doesn't fit with the so-called 'laws' of probability doesn't prove anything. You keep talking about laws as though that proved that it was true."

"Well, it doesn't *prove* that it's true, but the probability is so close to 100 percent that for all practical purposes, everybody agrees that it's true."

"Not everybody. Look at it this way: to you and me and most other people, including the scientists, it appears that entropy exists, because that's how it looks on *our* level of consciousness. But that's not necessarily how it looks to someone on a *higher* level of consciousness. Someone on a higher level of consciousness can see above all of the laws and the experiments. Maybe it looks completely different from a higher level of consciousness."

Since no one in the room claimed to be viewing the universe from a higher level of consciousness, Ken's statement terminated the debate. Perhaps Ken had merely intended to extricate himself by making an assertion to which Jeff could not reply. But the statement also carried a more sophisticated message: that there are many definitions of truth. Most of us have been brought up to believe in only one: the rational kind that can be proved, ideally even quantified, stated as a law on which everyone will agree. We are so accustomed to the rational variety, so certain of its uniqueness, that anyone who contradicts it is called a fool. But Ken, after a similar upbringing and a college education, has simply discarded that definition of truth. Not only does he doubt the second law of thermodynamics, but he has rejected the entire axiomatic structure on which it is based. One cannot even argue with him; there are no common postulates from which to start. One cannot even decide on the appropriate plane of consciousness from which to view the phenomenon.

Is Ken an isolated case? Listen to a few other examples. The next is a yoga practitioner in Cambridge, talking to a large audience:

"I just wanted to mention something before we hear our speaker tonight. I think most of us know how seriously the medical world misunderstands cancer, and I'm sure most of you are aware that we can do much better by ourselves. I have a book on the self-cure of cancer which I thought some of you would probably like to read or copy. If you're interested, I'll be in the back of the hall after the lecture."

Western medicine is also the culprit in this account from a Harvard student who is a follower of Guru Maharaj Ji:

"The problem with doctors in the West is that they don't understand anything about what produces health. They have almost no knowledge of nutrition, for instance, and they don't understand the energy fields which govern the functions of the human body. Their whole problem is that they are concerned with disease rather than with health. In China, acupuncturists are committed to maintaining health rather than curing disease. The knowledge from China is finally beginning to filter over here, but it will be a long time before most doctors in the United States begin to learn about the twelve energy fields and their function."

"Energy" is a favorite word among practitioners of Eastern disciplines, a word which is at once eminently technical and magnificently vague. Even those who appreciate its scientific meaning still use it loosely. The following is from a practitioner of Transcendental Meditation who has a college degree in physics:

> "After you meditate, it's very bad to take a shower, because meditation releases a very subtle energy field around your whole body. If you shower right after you meditate, you wash it off. So the thing to do is to shower *before* meditating."

The same person also explained to me that it was much better to sleep facing East than West, and that to face North was worst of all. When I asked him to explain, he began a complicated dissertation about the earth's magnetic field, with frequent references to "energy." Parenthetically — to anticipate a question from the psychiatrically trained reader — this person displayed no evidence of psychosis. Though he now works as an initiator in the TM organization, he worked previously as an engineer for a major aircraft manufacturer.

I also recall a dinner-table conversation with a Buddhist meditator. He told me of a friend who had eaten nothing but fruit for over twenty months.

> "Doesn't he drink milk or take vitamins, or anything?"

> "No. He eats absolutely nothing but fruit, and he drinks only fruit juices."

> "Well, if that were true, I'm almost certain he would be dead. Unless he ate twenty pounds of fruit a day, or something like that, he wouldn't be able to get enough of his essential amino acids and he would die of protein malnutrition."

> "Well, that may be true for you or me. *We* probably need all those amino acids to survive. But as you become a more evolved being, your need for protein becomes less and less. I'm sure you know that there are some very highly evolved yogis who haven't eaten anything for years and years. The point is that as you become more evolved, you become more and more in harmony with nature, and as a result, you lose your need for destructive things, such as killing animals or plants for food."

Another example, from a yoga practitioner named Keith:

"I worked as an aide in a mental hospital. You know, holding people down so they could be given shots, and making sure the door to the ward was locked, and all that sort of thing. But after sticking it out for a year, I left because I found that the doctors couldn't understand what was wrong with the patients at all. One time I heard them discussing whether this lady had a psychotic reactive depression or involutional melancholia, and I walked up and said, 'Have you considered the diagnosis of possession by evil spirits?' At first they thought I was joking, and when they realized that I was serious, they almost locked me up myself. They were just unwilling to accept anything outside their system."

Keith is suggesting the same thing as Ken: we in the West have come to assume, automatically, that the scientific approach is the legitimate one. A diagnosis of "involutional melancholia" is acceptable; "evil spirits" is not. And this despite the fact that African shamans, working with the latter hypothesis, reputedly achieve cure rates that compare favorably with our best mental institutions. And what about the poor lady with involutional melancholia? She is whisked into one of our hospitals, systematically prevented from committing suicide, and given Thorazine to suppress her psychotic ideation. After a course of eighteen shock treatments, she is promptly discharged on 300 mg. of Elavil a day: cured. Cured, at least, by any reasonable scientific criteria, improved on quantitative parameters, but somehow feeling short-changed. Perhaps she would feel better, even more human, if she had merited an elaborate ritual to exorcise her demons.

Finally, here is a segment from a dinner conversation with two Zen meditators:

"Did you know that it's possible to create chemical reactions just by contemplating the chemicals? I had a friend who was able to take some ordinary table salt and concentrate on it for an hour, and when he was through it contained traces of pure sodium and pure chlorine. It was broken down from the compound to the pure elements."

"How did he know that it contained sodium and chlorine?"

"He sent it to a lab for analysis. They'd never seen anything like it when they analyzed it, I guess. They must have thought he produced it in a cyclotron or something!"

If the reader has never heard actual meditators, he may be astonished by such quotations, perhaps even angered. It may sound ridiculously arrogant when a youth claims to be able to cure cancer, or extraordinarily superstitious for a former engineer to advocate sleeping in a given direction. But such views are spread far and wide in the Eastern subculture, throughout all of the various disciplines. To someone from the mainstream of our scientific culture, it is perhaps the most immediate, the most striking phenomenon that he will encounter among Eastern practitioners. He will hear hundreds of educated youths, youths who are clearly sane and rational in most of their everyday lives, repeatedly voicing beliefs that seem to date from the Middle Ages. Stepping into a group of dedicated meditators can be like entering a world where the scientific revolution has never occurred. If one is deeply attached to science, the experience may seem remarkably alien, even frightening.

Why have they discarded science? To begin with, they fear it. All of us do, to some extent, but the meditators' fear goes deeper. One reason has already emerged in the mercury-in-fish conversation in Chapter 3: modern technology is incomprehensible. Science has reached a level far beyond the knowledge of any single man. Just as one cannot simultaneously be ten thousand Ralph Naders, so one can understand only a minute piece of modern scientific knowledge. For the rest, one simply has to take on faith what the experts say. And if the experts are misinformed, or lying, or even out to destroy us, we have no way to tell. The meditators' doubts about food additives are a case in point. Who has not looked at the fine print on a supermarket can: "contains water, beef, tomato paste, sugar, soya lecithin, glutamic acid, nicotinic acid, sodium ascorbate, and pyrophosphate." It sounds terrible. Unless one is a doctor or a biochemist, there is no way to know that nicotinic acid is an essential B vitamin, sodium ascorbate synonymous with vitamin C, pyrophosphate a substance produced normally in the human body, glutamic acid a valuable amino acid, and soya lecithin a nutrient recommended by Adele Davis. Not all lists of ingredients are so benign of course, but the consumer has no way to distinguish which are benign and which are not. In this and hundreds of comparable daily situations, unless he is an expert himself in the particular field, he is helpless.

The meditators, as we have heard in many accounts, feel the helplessness acutely. And they deal with it, not merely by physical avoidance

— by rejecting processed foods, living away from the city, and simplifying their lives — but by intellectual denial of the scientific knowledge itself. The experts are simply wrong; they have no idea what they are talking about. The doctors misunderstand cancer, the psychiatrists do not appreciate mental disorders, the physicists are mistaken about entropy. This attitude is a very comforting one. It means that the experts are not so far ahead of the common man, that he is not at their mercy, because experts are more confused than he is. This defense is evident in a statement I once heard from a yoga practitioner in Boston:

"I don't know much about orthodox medicine, but I do understand about the different energy levels in the body, and how the different energies are carried by the blood corpuscles to the different layers of the nervous system and to the structures of the cerebral cortex. The main thing is eating foods with the right combination of energies that are capable of diffusing across the walls of the gastrointestinal tract. If you understand about the balance of energies and their effect on the cerebral cortex, you can keep yourself healthy and cure yourself of disease better than any doctors can . . . ."

He went on at some length to describe the energy levels, juxtaposing orthodox medical terminology with unorthodox beliefs. He spoke fairly loudly and quite rapidly, as though he were afraid that I might interrupt him. Though he did not know that I was a medical student, he had probably sensed that my views were more on the orthodox side. However, I felt that he was less interested in convincing me than in convincing himself. Like many other meditators, he seemed to be defending himself against a feeling of incompetence and helplessness. To concede that orthodox medicine is right is to admit that one has no choice but to trust the doctors. One can only hope that they know what they are doing, and that their motives are entirely humanitarian.

Not only has the information explosion made us pawns of the experts, but it has created an accelerating rate of change. As many observers have pointed out, the turnover rate of the world is becoming almost unbearably fast; machines, organizations, facts, values, and ideas become more and more rapidly obsolete. Alvin Toffler has used the term "future shock" to suggest that change is pushing the limits of human adaptability and taking an increasing toll in human happiness.

Modern American youths, especially, feel adrift in this change, unable to anchor themselves to a permanent philosophy.

The unplanned obsolescence of the drug subculture was, in many ways, a classic example of accelerating change. Much as some youths fantasized that it would preserve its integrity, they could only watch it dissolve in the face of commercialization, saturation coverage, and other forces of the Establishment. And amid that dissolution, once again, the East answered perfectly. Its timeless philosophy cannot be rendered obsolete; it cannot be reduced to a quantitative system comprehended only by the specialists. It is equally available to every man, and no amount of book learning or technical knowledge gives anyone an advantage. It offers an absolute in a sea of change, a vision which will not be disproved, replaced, outdated. Because its core is essentially abstract and mystical, its techniques unintellectual and even anti-intellectual, it is far less vulnerable to advancing science than more concrete Western theologies and philosophies. In fact, in our increasingly rationalistic, everything-can-be-explained world, the great Eastern systems are among the few surviving realms of human thought that are still invulnerable to science. What Darwin did to the Bible, Skinner to psychology, Masters and Johnson to human sexuality, cannot be done to the East. It is too supple; at every intellectual attack it steps aside, like a judo expert — even onto a different plane of consciousness.

Of course science has pecked and nibbled at the East. For several decades, psychophysiologists have toted their polygraphs to India and Japan to measure the EEGs and EKGs of the masters, and more recently a rash of studies has appeared in the United States. Some reasonably consistent and fairly impressive changes have been found. It is beginning to appear, for example, that highly experienced practitioners in several different disciplines — persons who have perhaps reached "cosmic consciousness" or its equivalent — produce theta waves (waves with a frequency of five to seven cycles per second) on their electroencephalograms. Since theta waves are almost never seen on the EEGs of ordinary adults, the finding is suggestive. But even allowing that cosmic consciousness can someday be measured with theta waves, the state of mind behind the waves, the wisdom and understanding that it may represent, its essence, is still untouched.

Some meditators are intrigued by such things as the theta wave findings, hoping that it may support the cause of Eastern disciplines. But in general they are skeptical of probing scientists. They are proud of the mystical and anti-intellectual basis of their techniques, aware of their remoteness from science, and determined to keep it that way. I have encountered this personally on several occasions: when I revealed to some groups of meditators the mere fact that I was a medical student, I sometimes felt a subtle change in the tenor of the conversation. They became just slightly less friendly than before, slightly more defensive, more hesitant to voice their thoughts and views.

A MISSING VITAMIN

We are approaching a deeper issue in meditators' feelings about science. Beyond the esoterica and constant obsolescence that science induces, it spoils things, structuralizes and demythologizes things, deprives them of their life and their magic. Meditators sense this: the phenomenon that the poet referred to when he wrote "the knower petrifies the known."

One amusing description of this occurred during lunch at a Transcendental Meditation course. We had just heard Maharishi Mahesh Yogi lecture about the analogy between the growth of personal potential and the growth of a garden. It is not necessary to condition the individual petals and leaves of each of the flowers; instead one "waters the root and enjoys the fruit." In other words, if the mind is nurtured by regular meditation, individual potentials will improve automatically. We were talking about the garden analogy.

> "I wonder what would happen to the garden if a big American corporation got hold of it?" someone said.
> "First they'd call in a team of leaf scientists and another team of petal scientists, and everyone would disagree on what was best to do. Then they'd give it artificial light to make it grow faster. And add chemicals to the soil."
> "No," said another. "They'd remove the soil entirely and grow it completely on chemical fertilizers. Then they would take it indoors and water it artificially instead of using rain."
> "Then give it X rays or something to make the plants into mutants so that they'd grow bigger."

"Not to mention pesticides, of course. They couldn't possibly grow the plants without pesticides."

"And then they'd get pollution inside the building where the garden was kept, and they'd have to bring in another team of experts to install antipollution equipment to keep the pollution down."

"Yes, but the garden would start to die anyway, because they had left out a necessary nutrient in the artificial fertilizer. So then they'd call in a team of plant nutritionists to find out what vitamin was missing from the soil. But before they could find out what vitamin was missing the plants would all have died."

A fanciful description, to be sure, but uncomfortably close to the state of affairs in some areas of modern technology. And not only in technology, but modern thought as well: the rationalistic worldview has deprived the psyche of something that it needs, a vitamin essential for its well-being. Much as meditators feel that modern processed foods have been deprived of natural nutrients, so they more dimly sense that a spiritual vitamin has been lost in scientific information-processing. In different words, they have come to the age-old realization that man cannot live by bread alone — even the "enriched" variety. (This, incidentally, has been scientifically proved, two thousand years after it was said: if rats are fed an exclusive diet of white supermarket bread, they all die of vitamin deficiencies.)

What is it that is missing? What human need has been left unsatisfied? Carl Jung might have called it the need for myth; in one essay, he suggested that it perhaps accounted for many sightings of flying saucers. The usual circular shape of the saucers, he pointed out, recalls the *mandala*, a circular Eastern symbol of totality, wholeness. Aldous Huxley's savage, in *Brave New World*, could only describe his need as "the right to be unhappy." Others say that now God is dead, and we feel a need for religion. Whatever it may be called, most of us are aware of a deficit, and there is evidence that it is growing. Look at the characters of recent fiction and nonfiction: Black Elk, Don Juan of the Castaneda trilogy, Jonathan Livingston Seagull. They all speak of something beyond the rational, a spiritual, mystical plane of reality above the drabness of the "real" world. And perhaps it reflects a spreading dissatisfaction with that drabness that we have made these books into best-sellers. We miss the mythical, the supernatural, the unexplainable. An emptiness is left when magic is made obsolete.

Of course technology has tried to satisfy us with its own brand of magic, the sixteen-track-studio variety where anything is possible at a touch of the controls. When youths flirted with drugs and the light show, they sampled their share of that magic, too. But it ultimately proved to be a pale kind of magic, a poor substitute for the real thing. Having discovered that, they looked, quite naturally, to the East. The very word conjures images of magic: snake charmers, fire walkers, fakirs performing impossible feats of mind over matter. The East is a veritable storehouse of magic, an endless source of things that science cannot explain.

A striking example of this is the book *Autobiography of a Yogi* by Paramahansa Yogananda, an Eastern master who brought Kriya Yoga to the United States a generation ago. The book is popular and highly regarded among not only yoga practitioners, but youths in many other Eastern disciplines. A look at some of the chapter titles suggests why: "The Saint with Two Bodies," "The Levitating Saint," "The Sleepless Saint," "Materializing a Palace in the Himalayas," "The Woman Yogi Who Never Eats," and so forth. The book is overflowing with accounts of miracles, but the first one, concerning the master Lahiri Mahasaya, is the best:

> It appears that the Master had an aversion to being photo-
> graphed. Over his protest, a picture was once taken of him
> and a group of devotees, including Kali Kumar Roy. It was
> an amazed photographer who discovered that the plate, which
> had clear images of all the disciples, revealed nothing more
> than a blank space in the center where he had reasonably ex-
> pected to find the outlines of Lahiri Mahasaya. The phenome-
> non was widely discussed.
>
> A student who was an expert photographer, Ganga Dhar
> Babu, boasted that the fugitive figure would not escape him.
> The next morning, as the guru sat in lotus posture on a
> wooden bench with a screen behind him, Ganga Dhar Babu
> arrived with his equipment. Taking every precaution for
> success, he greedily exposed twelve plates. On each one he
> soon found the imprint of the wooden bench and screen,
> but once again the master's form was missing.

Humbled, Ganga Dhar Babu went before the master. After some hours, Lahiri Mahasaya finally spoke:

"I am Spirit. Can your camera reflect the omnipresent Invisible?"

"I see it cannot! But, Holy Sir, I lovingly desire a picture of your bodily temple. My vision has been narrow; until today I did not realize that in you the Spirit fully dwells."

"Come, then, tomorrow morning. I will pose for you." Again the photographer focused his camera. This time the sacred figure, not cloaked with mysterious imperceptibility, was sharp on the plate.

Several meditators have cited this to me as their favorite account in the book. And little wonder; it is a direct confrontation between science and magic, with the latter emerging victorious. Photographically speaking, the knower, for once, failed to petrify the known.

For many youths, magical feats represent one of the most intriguing possibilities of Eastern disciplines. They offer the hope of beating science at its own game, on its own territory. The self-cure of cancer is such a case: how satisfying it would be to disenthrone all the oncologists in a single blow! Most Eastern practitioners do not go quite so far in their beliefs, but practically all agree that highly advanced yogis can perform feats that would be deemed impossible by Western physiologists. And in some disciplines, particularly Transcendental Meditation, experiments are underway to test this. Probably the most famous is that of Wallace (1970), which found a 16 percent decrease in oxygen consumption during Transcendental Meditation. This decrease is greater than that which occurs in sleep, hypnosis, or even autonomic conditioning with biofeedback. In other words, science knows of no way to duplicate the phenomenon. Transcendental Meditators were jubilant when the study appeared, not only because it gave support for their cause, but because it meant that they possessed something that science did not entirely understand.

A number of similar studies have appeared (see reference notes), many of them performed by scientists who were themselves practitioners of Eastern disciplines. On a superficial level, the studies may appear as attempts to subsume Eastern disciplines to science. But in reading the studies, particularly those with spectacular results, one gets the opposite impression: the experimenter (not to mention the subjects) seems to have fervently hoped to come up with something that would overthrow a few of the cherished beliefs of physiologists, psychologists, or doctors. This is not to say that such studies are necessarily severely biased or poorly controlled, but merely that the experimenters, like most of us, were conspicuously searching for a way to shake up established scientific theory.

In other words, even if the fakirs were shown to be fakers (but they are far too elusive to permit that, of course) and even if it were found that Paramahansa Yogananda indulged in a bit of hyperbole, there is still hope for putting science on the defensive — right in its own laboratories. The East will not be easily defeated. In a later generation, perhaps, science will manage to process and petrify Eastern wisdom, desiccate its richness. But for now, millions of practitioners stand ready to defend it, to guard its magic, its mystery, its spiritual power.

MADNESS AND THE TYRANNY OF THE EGO

But not only have meditators rejected science, and even doubted rationalistic philosophy, the basis of science, but many have gone a step beyond that: they have questioned the seat of rationality itself, the ego. They have doubted our entire Western concept of what is sanity and what is madness.

It began, once again, in the drug world. As an introduction, let me recall another character from *Voices from the Drug Culture*, named Bert, who had already become a Zen meditator at the time that that book was written (see p. 67). Before he took up Zen, Bert was a heavy drug user in prep school. Reproduced here is his account of sniffing glue in those days:

> "Well, we went downtown and bought a model kit and a thing of glue. The model kit was just an excuse so that the guy in the store wouldn't ask questions. Then you put the glue in a paper bag and cover your face with it, and start breathing. After a minute or two you start feeling a little drunk, and then you suddenly realize that with every breath you are getting further and further from reality. And after a few more breaths, there is absolutely nothing — no past, present, future, time, meaning, existence — just

nothing. What happened to me was that I ran screaming down the corridor and down the stairs and I started pounding on my faculty adviser's door. Then I collapsed on the floor. He came out, looked around, didn't look down, and miraculously closed the door without seeing me. I guess he must have thought it was a bunch of guys pounding on his door and then running away. At any rate, I was beginning to come to my senses by that point, and I realized how close I'd come to getting kicked out of the school."

"Why did you do glue in the first place?"

"Just to blow my mind, I guess."

Why would Bert want simply to blow his mind? Why would he intentionally go stark raving mad? And Bert is not alone. Hundreds of thousands of youths have tried mind-blowing drugs such as glue, nitrous oxide, and a whole range of other volatile liquids. Even some of the hallucinogens, especially the belladonna alkaloids, are popular not because they are pleasurable (they are more often downright unpleasant) but for the sheer experience of utter insanity that they produce. The belladonna user holds conversations with nonexistent people, smokes nonexistent cigarettes, and replies to questions with a chain of *non sequiturs*:

"Do you want to go to dinner?"

"No, not really. I've never liked ice cream sandwiches, but if you go down to the Amazon basin, where they import the blue polka-dotted things that Dr. McLaren . . . . I mean, if you like ice cream you probably wouldn't put peanut butter on it, but peanut butter is really the only . . . . What was I just saying? I've forgotten."

Often one has total amnesia for the belladonna experience afterward. Yet I have met some youths who have tried belladonna or glue a dozen times. Why would anyone not only deliberately make himself insane, but go back to it again and again? Is there something wrong with sanity, something slightly stifling about it, that so many youths should want to escape from under it? For that matter, is there conceivably something wrong with our whole definition of sanity? Perhaps there is a morsel of truth in the classic graffiti slogan that "reality is a crutch."

In recent years, a number of Western writers have begun to question orthodox ideas about sanity. Alan Watts has suggested that possibly the Western definition of sanity is itself insane. Szasz and others have

pointed to the mythology underlying the term "mental illness."
And R. D. Laing, particularly, has convincingly revealed how tenuous is
our distinction between sanity and madness, and how dubious are the
value-judgments allied to these words. The man in the street will not necessarily agree with such commentators, but he will quip that "the world
is insane nowadays." And in an age of thermonuclear weapons, nerve
gas, and germ warfare, it is hard to take that statement entirely in jest.

Some meditators have read Laing or Szasz or Watts, but most of
them have begun to ask questions on their own. Though they may not
know what "the ego" means in psychoanalytic terminology, they have
come to identify that part of their minds as something not entirely desirable. They see the ego as not merely a servant, essential for coping
with the surrounding environment, but a tyrant which suppresses spon-
taneity, love, vision, spiritual understanding. Usually their belief is not
that clearly formulated, of course. It is more often expressed as a vague
sense that something is missing, that something of value is lost if one
follows the path of total "sanity." I can remember a number of occasions on which the subject arose during conversations among meditators.
For example, listen to one Transcendental Meditator:

"You know, I wouldn't mind being insane. I think it
might be sort of interesting to be psychotic. I think that
psychotic people may be a lot more spiritually enlightened
than we are."

"I've seen a lot of them, and they usually didn't look
very blissful to me," I replied.

"Well, I'm sure it's not true of all psychotic people. The
difference is that they freaked out because society just blew
their minds and they couldn't cope with it. They're on the
defensive against society, so they're not happy. But suppose
you just politely said to society, 'Well, I'm tired of your way
of looking at the world!' and you just went insane on purpose, if you see what I mean. I'd sort of like to do that in a
way."

Another example, from a yoga practitioner:

"You know about a year ago I was seeing a psychiatrist
and he was prescribing me *Thorazine* for what I later realized were flashes of cosmic consciousness! Since then I've
stopped seeing him, of course."

Or from a practitioner of Tibetan Buddhism:

> "I think the great task that we all face on the path to en-
> lightenment is just defeating our own egos."

Where did meditators get such a bad opinion of the ego? In addition
to their drug experiences and their knowledge of recent psychological
literature, they seem to have formed a link between their idea of the ego
and their idea of adulthood as described in Chapter 5. To succumb to
adulthood, or rather to the stifling conformism which they perceive as
adulthood, means to allow the tyranny of the ego to become complete.
It is to relinquish all that is good about being a child: the openness,
naturalness, and ingenuousness, and live instead under an iron regime of
rationality. To enthrone the ego, they believe, is to sacrifice the best
aspects of being human.

Their belief is based not only on their conception of adulthood, but
on that supreme experience of regression to early childhood: LSD. For
LSD, as I have suggested previously (*Voices from the Drug Culture,*
p. 48), has a "pedomimetic" effect: it transports the user into a state
closely resembling the first years of childhood. One reason for this, as
Aldous Huxley and other writers have suggested, may be that LSD impairs
the brain's usual mechanism for censoring "trivial" sensory input in the interest of efficiency. One would be paralyzed if he were constantly dis-
tracted, as a child is, by the color of flowers, the beauty of the sky, the
sound of the wind. Therefore the adult ego screens out such material
so that we can concentrate on our daily tasks. But with LSD, one is
"turned on" to these stimuli again; one is laid open to every detail of
the surrounding environment. Suddenly the most trivial things seem remarkable, extraordinarily beautiful, even holy. And this experience of
childish wonderment, as many writers (again including Huxley) have suggested, is strikingly similar to that described by Eastern mystics who
have reached enlightenment. Listen:

> "I went to select a record to play on the stereo. Sudden-
> ly I was overcome with the simple fact that I was selecting a
> record. It was the most wonderful thing in the universe, that
> *I* could be selecting a record. It was miraculous. I felt that I
> was God, that I should be entitled to select a record. I be-
> came so intoxicated with the feeling that I never actually
> played the record, but simply marveled at the sheer joy of
> selecting it."

The second quotation is shorter:

> How wondrously supernatural,
> And how miraculous this!
> I draw water, and I carry fuel!

The latter quotation is more poetic, but otherwise the two express an identical sensation: an overwhelming, childlike amazement with what are normally considered banal experiences. The first is from a former college roommate of mine, just after he first tried LSD. The second is from the Zen master P'ang Yun, and is one of the great classics of Japanese haiku.

I need not belabor such comparisons, for many have been published before (see reference notes), some even more strikingly similar than the above. The point is merely that meditators have good reason to perceive an analogy between the egolessness of childhood (though it may be chemically simulated), and profound mystic experiences. In fact it was a Western master, previously quoted in this chapter, who said, "except ye be as little children, ye cannot enter the Kingdom of Heaven." Again, two thousand years later, a supportive scientific finding has emerged: children, like the masters, but unlike ordinary adults, produce theta waves on their EEGs.

Of course none of these various quotations and scraps of evidence actually proves the equation of egolessness, childhood, LSD, madness, and enlightenment, although taken as a whole, the evidence is certainly suggestive. It is assembled here, not as proof, but merely to give an idea of some of the thoughts and reasoning in the minds of many practitioners of Eastern disciplines. They have decided, in short, that rationality is not so all-important as our society would suggest, and that the ego is not entirely benign, but the overgrown child of a hyperrational age. They have reasoned that "I" and "self" are not the sacred entities we suppose them to be. After all, it is hard to continue boasting their primacy after seeing them obliterated with 0.0003 grams of LSD or a few breaths of vapor. Tenuous creatures indeed, the "self" and the "I"; perhaps, many meditators have concluded, they are only illusions. But to discard the self as an illusion — isn't this called madness?

If the reader will permit a few more tantalizing bits of evidence, he may find that the link between the East and what we call madness is even closer than he might suspect. Consider for example the well-known "double-bind" theory of schizophrenia (Bateson *et al*, 1956), which holds that schizophrenia is produced when a child constantly receives contradictory messages from an authority figure, but has no way of resolving the contradiction or stepping outside of it. An example is the mother who verbally asserts her love to the child, while simultaneously broadcasting hate and disgust through physical gestures. A large number of schizophrenics prove to have endured such a double-bind situation in childhood.

Now the basis of Zen meditation, the *Koan*, is nothing more than a double bind. Here are two examples from Watts (1958):

> A long time ago a man kept a goose in a bottle. It grew larger and larger until it could not get out of the bottle anymore; he did not want to break the bottle nor did he wish to hurt the goose; how would you get it out?

> Here is a man on a tree holding one of the branches in his mouth, but neither clinging to any of them with his hands nor touching the trunk with his feet. Someone at the foot of the tree asks him, "What is Zen?" If he does not answer the question, he cannot satisfy the man, but if he speaks, even a word, he will at once fall down to death. At such a moment, what answer would you make if you were he?

A Zen disciple must spend years meditating on such a Koan, and even during his daily work he is urged to keep his mind affixed to the Koan as much as possible. Imagine spending five years in constant concentration on a double bind: The analogy to Bateson is inescapable. Is Zen simply a programmed way to go schizophrenic? Watts, in a later work (1961), recognizes the analogy, but is careful to distinguish the two:

> But in liberation this comes to pass not through an unconscious compulsion (as in schizophrenia) but through insight, through understanding and breaking the double bind which society imposes.

Watts's distinction is very reasonable, of course, but isn't it possible that in both double-bind situations, the same chemical or neurological "click" occurs? In the former case the click occurs in an immature mind under the most adverse conditions; in the latter, it occurs in a carefully prepared mind under supportive conditions. But speaking in terms of pure physiology, are the clicks perhaps identical? Perhaps Thorazine *would* suppress cosmic consciousness!

Zen is not the only technique that sounds schizophrenic to the Western ear. Ask the average man what would happen to him if he spent ten years meditating in a cave, and he will probably say that he would go mad. Left alone to contemplate life without the usual narcotics of society, activity, and theology, we would all go "insane." Isn't life itself, as suggested by existential psychoanalysis, a giant double bind? On one level we act as though it were all meaningful, but on another we are born and dead within a second, an infinitesimal speck on the scale of cosmic time. What is the truly sane response to that dilemma, or is there one?

But we are straying into philosophy. Returning to pharmacology, listen to Richard Alpert's account (1971) of giving LSD to his guru in India:

> He looked at me and extended his hand. So I put into his hand what's called a "white Lightning." This is an LSD pill and this one was from a special batch that had been made specially for me for traveling. And each pill was 305 micrograms, and very pure. Very good acid. Usually you start a man over 60, maybe with 50 to 75 micrograms, very gently, so you won't upset him. 300 of pure acid is a very solid dose.
>
> He looks at the pill and extends his hand further. So I put a second pill — that's 610 micrograms — then a third pill — that's 915 micrograms — into his palm.
>
> That is sizeable for a first dose for anyone!
>
> "Ah-cha."
>
> And he swallows them! I see them go down. There's no doubt. And that little scientist in me says, "This is going to be very interesting!"
>
> All day long I'm there, and every now and then he twinkles at me and nothing nothing happens! That was his answer to my question. Now you have the data I have.

Now there are only two classes of people known to Western science who do not get high on LSD: people who are missing their left temporal lobe and — schizophrenics.

Is Alpert's guru schizophrenic? Does he have *soma* in his veins, as the Vedas say, or merely abnormal catecholamine metabolites? Does he speak cryptic wisdom or loose associations? Does he possess equanimity or flatness of affect? God-consciousness or delusions of grandeur? Furthermore, does it matter? And even if it did matter, could you possibly determine it? On which level of consciousness would we agree to begin? The definitions collapse; science, sanity, madness, and magic coalesce into a blur.

Later in Alperts' book appears a picture of a door. On it is written:

MAGIC THEATRE
FOR MADMEN ONLY
PRICE OF ADMISSION:
YOUR MIND

Are some meditators sacrificing their sanity for a glimpse of the magic? Perhaps not, but they have sacrificed much of science, including the most basic postulates on which science is built, and even ventured into that vague and forbidden territory on the border of what we call madness, in the hopes of finding something beautiful, something more satisfying, beyond.

8/ SEARCHING FOR THE SPHERE

We come now to the highest level of abstraction: the philosophical reasons for starting on the road East. Of course, few youths, if any, begin Eastern disciplines for *purely* philosophical reasons; invariably some emotional reactions lurk behind the more idealistic ones. But this is not in any way to demean the philosophers I have met among meditators, for many of them offered striking insights into both the East and the West, and sophisticated reasons for their decisions. The philosophical elite of meditators represents only a tiny fraction of the total group. Nevertheless, it is well worth listening to some of them, because often they manage to verbalize ideas which exist in the minds of many other meditators, but which are rarely expressed. They are spokesmen for the ideals of the larger group.

The philosophers are not necessarily the most advanced or enlightened of meditators, for intellectual skill rarely aids progress in Eastern disciplines, and may even hamper it. They are merely the most eloquent speakers. The following three accounts are presented, then, not so much because they offer new material, but because they seem too colorful to omit entirely.

The first is a biochemistry graduate student in Massachusetts named Earle, who has practiced what he calls "home-grown Zen" for three years:

"I think the greatest illusion we all grow up with is that the whole game of life is so serious. Our parents, society, Western religion — they all give us the idea that we have to *do* something with our lives, accomplish something. My parents believed that, and they taught it to me. They never even questioned it. And in retrospect, that's not surprising. My dad worked his way through medical school on his own money in the heart of the Depression. Then he took an internship and residency where he got paid about fifty dollars a month or something ridiculous like that, so that my mother had to support him by working as a legal secretary for five years. They were far too busy to stop and think about whether it was serious or not. They didn't have time for any nonsense like that. It was out of the question.

"And so my dad finally started practice and became a great doctor. He practiced for twenty years and one day three years ago while he was driving to the office in the morning he died of a heart attack. It must have hit him almost instantly, because he fell unconscious while driving right in the middle of the street, and the car just quietly drove off into the bushes with him lying on the seat. In fact, I saw the car before they took it away. It looked strange, just sitting in the bushes, as though it had decided to revolt against the commands of its master and drive where it pleased instead. The whole scene, seeing the car just sitting there, had a strange effect on me that I can't really describe.

"About a month afterward I was talking with a neighbor who was the same age as my father, and the subject got around to his death, and we exchanged the usual remarks about wasn't-it-a-tragedy and was-it-really-worth-working-that-hard-all-your-life and what-does-life-all-mean-anyhow, and so forth. And it struck me that most of us, like my father, simply postpone thinking about what it all means, and we keep ourselves busy, and keep ourselves convinced that what we're doing is serious, just because it's too frightening to stop and wonder if it all does mean anything or if it *is* serious. I really started wondering about that.

"I don't think my father postponed those questions just because he was frightened. I think that, deep down, he had some sort of subconscious belief that he would be *rewarded* for working so hard. I think the fundamental belief he had was that there is a life after death. So that even if you spent your entire life toiling away, and died before you could enjoy your retirement, it was O.K., because you would still be able to relax and have fun in eternity! I'm not saying that Dad was a religious man. He never went to church. But I still think that on a subconscious level, the life-after-death idea was still with him as much as it was with our Puritan fathers. In fact, I find it hard to imagine that all the people in our society would take it all so seriously if they were convinced, instead, that death was the *end* and after that they would not exist. Do you see what I'm saying? If you really *knew* for sure that it would be all over when you died, completely all over, then being happy *now* would suddenly seem more important and accomplishing something would somehow seem a lot less important.

"So I think Christianity had a lot to do with the 'seriousness' illusion. Not so much Christ himself. He was a pretty hip guy. He pointed out that the lilies of the field didn't have to work to get rewarded. But after Christ, Christianity gradually acquired a more and more sober, unenlightened quality, culminating in Calvinism and Puritanism and things like that. And that soberness and seriousness has come right down to the present day.

"I don't claim to have escaped that, obviously. Next year I'll probably be studying nucleic-acid metabolism in the salivary gland of the giant Amazonian earthworm or something equally absurd, and acting like it's important. But I've had several things my father didn't have. First, there's been a little more dilution of religion between my father's generation and mine; I've been fed less of it than he. I still probably believe the life-after-death assumption on a deep subconscious level, but not as much as he did. Secondly, I've been exposed to a lot of Eastern literature that was simply not available in the West before. But I think the most important thing is that my family was rich. I was brought up in a situation where any conceivable need would be taken care of and where I didn't have to worry about the future. And so I've had a lot of time to stop and think about what it all means. *Time* is the one thing that is most different. I've had so much more

time than my father was ever allowed, just to be able to contemplate things without worrying about immediate issues.
And when you have money and you have time, the old Puritan philosophy just doesn't sound as convincing as it did in
previous centuries. It doesn't have the punch it used to have.

"And that's where Zen came into my life. Even though it's
very old, it's also a very modern philosophy. It fits in perfectly
for thousands of kids who have had the time to stop and think,
and who have realized that maybe the seriousness philosophy
and the Protestant ethic aren't quite up to date anymore. By
that I don't mean that those kids have decided to be lazy or im-
moral. They're simply learning to 'play the game of life without taking it seriously,' as Alan Watts says. And it's not as if
they're all planning to go off to a monastery in Japan or Tibet
and spend five years in meditation. I think most of them are
like me. They just started reading a few books, snooping
around here and there, and they discovered the East as
something whose time has come, something that really
fitted in with their feelings and their needs today."

Earl had no plans to go to the East himself when he said this, but two
months ago, having obtained his Ph.D. in biochemistry, he left for Japan
to spend the summer. I have not heard from him; perhaps he has found
a monastery where he can experience Zen more intensely.

The second account is from Ellie, already quoted in Chapter 4, des-
cribing LSD trips during her Haight-Ashbury years:

"I was already looking for something before I even tried
acid. I already knew that there was something *there*, something more to be discovered. So I set about trying acid very
seriously. As a matter of fact I started with acid. I had never
taken alcohol or marijuana before I took acid. Not only that,
but I deliberately started with a huge dose — close to two
thousand mikes — rather than building up from little doses.
The only preparation I had was reading books about acid. I
read all the classic books, like Leary's book based on the
Tibetan Book of the Dead, and stuff by Aldous Huxley, and
so forth. So I was prepared to have a really mystic experience
from the start.

"But when I actually tried acid for the first time, instead

of having beautiful visions, I had a bad trip. I hallucinated bugs crawling across the floor, and thought that my friends were going to desert me, and got scared that I'd never come down — the whole bag. But I came down, after about twelve hours. And what I realized was that I had been trying to fight it, and that's why I had had a bad trip. Deep down I had expected to preserve my sanity, my rationality. In other words, the trip would begin, and my mind would look down and contemplate the trip and say, 'Ah, how interesting!' I guess I had the idea that there was some part of my brain that was sacred, some piece of rationality that could not be touched by the acid. And when the acid began to come on, and when I realized that even the highest reaches of my mind were themselves susceptible to the acid, and that *everything* in my brain was going to go under, I panicked. I tried to fight to preserve my rationality, and of course the more I fought the more irrational it all became, and pretty soon there was nothing left of me, no 'me' at all. But even *then* I tried to fight it. I was a real fighter in those days. And so I had twelve hours of sheer horror, the worst horror I'd ever had in my life. I wanted to die, I thought of committing suicide, everything.

"After it was over, I had a very strange reaction. I wanted to do acid again, as soon as possible. Something inside told me that that first experience had been necessary, that it was inevitable that I should have had it. And suddenly I realized that the worst possible time to *stop* taking acid was right then, that I had to do it again right away, before I could reassemble all my defenses and retreat back into the uptight rationality scene that I had been in before. So I deliberately took another 2,000-mike dose the next weekend. And as it came on, I suddenly understood how to take it, and the whole trip was indescribably beautiful. I learned more from that first pair of trips than I did from the next two hundred or three hundred."

"But why did you even dare to take it a second time, after such a bad first trip? It's hard to believe."

"Because I realized that the bad first trip was not the

acid's fault, but my fault. And that if I didn't go back and do acid a second time, I'd be making the same mistakes for the rest of my life. It wasn't even *my* fault, really. You know whose fault it was? It was Aristotle's fault, and Descartes's fault. Those two guys were responsible for my bad trip. The reason I say that is that I grew up with an implicit belief in the mind-body duality. I believed, just like everybody else, that your mind is different from your body, that it's higher than your body, and that they just have connection lines running between them. That alienation of mind from body is something most people take for granted. There's even a subtle sort of pride about it, the idea that your mind is somehow up there, untouchable, almost as if it wasn't part of the real world. In other words, even though you believe that your body is just part of the world, you still treat your mind like something special and separate. You alienate *yourself* from the world that way, if you see what I mean. And with me, it took two thousand mikes of acid for twelve hours to shatter that pride."

"But you continued to take acid for two or three hundred times after that?"

"Two or three times a week for more than two years. As I said before, I was really serious about it. And during all that time, I practically never had another bad trip. A few bad moments here and there, perhaps, but generally all good trips."

"Why did you keep taking acid for so long?"

"Because I wanted to gain a permanent kind of vision from it, to get some sort of permanent understanding. But I always came down. I could never capture the feeling I had from acid on a permanent basis. And so, obviously, I started looking more and more to the East. I read everything I could get my hands on — Ouspensky, Meher Baba, the *Gita*, the *Tao Te Ching*, and the Bible, too. But the book that really turned me on was *Autobiography of a Yogi*, by Paramahansa Yogananda. Then I started reading all of his other books, and one day I realized that I had found the path in the form of Kriya Yoga. And that day I stopped taking LSD, and I've taken it

only once since. What I realized is that I had been using LSD
as sort of a mechanized way to get to cosmic consciousness,
as though it was an airplane that would automatically carry
me there. It's only reasonable that I had that misconception,
because I am a part of a mechanized age where everything is
performed automatically. But I don't regret having done LSD
all that time. It was a necessary step. It opened the door to
me and showed me a whole universe beyond the one that I
know. Getting there through Kriya Yoga may take a long
time, but I'll get there, eventually."

What is the thing that Ellie seeks? How was she so certain of its existence that she was not even deterred by a horrible experience with LSD?
Few meditators have tried to put into words the thing that Ellie called
"something more to be discovered"; they are content to call it cosmic
consciousness, self-realization, enlightenment, or *satori*. It exists, they
are quite sure, but it is nonverbal by its very nature, an essence which
cannot be reduced to words.

The following account, written in a letter from a Transcendental Meditator named Chuck, tries to convey that essence in an indirect way. The
story, curiously enough, occurred to him in a dream, just before he awakened in the morning, and he promptly wrote it down, with some embel-
lishments, on paper.

You are a two-dimensional creature living on a plane.
You are a happy creature, relatively comfortable, in good
health. You have many friends among the other two-dimensional creatures who inhabit the plane, and you have
traveled far and wide on its surface. All in all, you consider
yourself quite a clever little creature. You have been every-
where, seen everything, tried everything, and generally you
feel rather self-satisfied. Occasionally, you have a transient
funny feeling that perhaps there ought to be something more,
somewhere, to life, but this does not bother you very often.
And so you continue to travel contentedly around the plane.
One day, someone you've never seen before comes up to you
and says, "You know what? There's a thing called a sphere!"

"What does it look like?" you say.

"Well, I can't describe it to you. There's no way I can define it using your terms."

"What do you mean?" you ask, a bit irritated. "What does it look like — a triangle, a square, a circle?"

"It looks definitely more like a circle than either a triangle or a square, but for me to say even that is misleading in a way, because, actually, it doesn't look like a circle at all!"

"Stop all this mumbo-jumbo and just explain to me straightforwardly what it is."

"I'm sorry, I can't."

"Sounds to me like it doesn't exist at all, or if it does, *you* sure as hell have never seen one. I mean, do you seriously expect me to believe all this drivel?"

"No, of course you don't have to believe it if you don't want to. I had just thought that you might be interested, that's all." He starts to walk away.

Something, somewhere deep inside you, tells you that he is right.

"Hey, just a minute," you say. "Suppose there is such a thing as a sphere. How do I find it?"

He replies, but his explanation of how to find the sphere is so far-out and bizarre, so incongruent with what any rational creature knows, that you wonder if maybe the guy shouldn't be locked up in a hospital or something. You scoff at him some more, and he goes away.

But, as time passes, you find yourself haunted by the possibility of the sphere. It lingers on in your mind, even when you should be thinking of other things. Sometimes, when you have some time off from your work elsewhere on the plane, you do a little research about it: read books, talk to others, make forays up and down the plane in search of it. You even undertake a long trip, farther up and farther down the plane than you have ever gone before — but it still comes to naught.

One day, much later, you meet him again.

"I've been thinking about what you said long ago," you say to him, "and I've come to the guarded conclusion that you *may* be right. But I've traveled far and wide, and I haven't found anything. How do I find the sphere?"

"Actually, you don't have to travel at all. As a matter of fact, your chances of discovering it as you are sitting right here are just as great as if you traveled to a great distance. It doesn't matter where you are."

"How do I find it, then?"

He begins the same sort of vague description he gave before.

"What is this you mean about my having to discard all my previous assumptions? How am I supposed to do that?"

"Well, let me give you an analogy that perhaps will be meaningful to you. You must forgive my habit of speaking in analogies, but it is the best way. Have you ever had the sensation of trying to fall asleep when you can't? You desperately want to get a full eight hours of sleep, and you keep trying to force yourself to fall asleep promptly, readjusting the pillow, changing your position, counting sheep, but it doesn't work. Periodically you glance at the clock beside your bed, and more time has passed, but you are still trying to fall asleep. Eventually, you get so tired of trying to fall asleep that, for a moment, you forget to try, and suddenly — you fall asleep. Discovering the sphere is rather like that. Just at the moment when you have exerted all your efforts, exhausted every one of your familiar tricks, at the moment where nothing seems to have worked and you just give up trying, suddenly you succeed! Can you see what I mean?"

"I *think* so."

"Good. I'm delighted to hear that you are interested. You will have many setbacks in your search, needless to say, and at times you'll swear that the whole thing is a hoax, but if you persist in your faith, you'll ultimately find the sphere. And when you find the sphere, a whole new world of understanding will open to you, *instantly.* Everything in that new world is so vast that, by comparison, the plane on which you now exist will seem vanishingly small by comparison.

"With all my heart, I wish you good luck, and every chance for success!"

And so your search begins.

The idea that somewhere there really is a sphere, that there exists something more to be found beyond the confines of the everyday world, a mystical dimension orthogonal to the plane of rationality — this belief in one form or another is shared by almost all of the youths who have turned to the East. Of course, to some extent it is a universal belief: everyone, in backyard-fence conversations or in solitude, has asked what it all means, and wondered if there is something more. But most of us are content merely to ask the question occasionally, then dismiss it and return to our daily routine. Earle, Ellie, and Chuck are not: to them the question has become too acute, too important to ignore. They have become so convinced of the third dimension that they have set out to find it in a systematic way.

What convinced them? Many meditators feel that they have actually the sphere on LSD, as Ellie did; now they are merely trying to ture that vision by nonchemical means. But Ellie, like many of the other philosophical meditators, was intellectually convinced even before she began taking LSD, so convinced that a bad trip did not deter her. Much of her faith she acquired through works by Huxley, Leary, Watts, and other writers who have investigated both psychedelic and Eastern mystical experiences: an expanding literature which only a generation ago, as Earle pointed out, was practically nonexistent. But the interest of Ellie and Earle seemed to stem less from the positive reinforcement of the mystical writers than from a sense of having exhausted all of the other possibilities. Affluence, college educations, modern transportation, communication, and other technological advances, experience in the drug culture, and most of all, a prolonged youth with minimal responsibilities, had already permitted them an extraordinarily wide range of experimentation. They had enjoyed opportunities, unequaled in any other culture or any previous generation, to investigate every physical and intellectual realm on earth — even within their own brains. Not that they were smarter than their predecessors or their contemporaries in other societies; they simply possessed the means to test things more rapidly. Whether it was a curse or a blessing, they experienced an unprecedented turnover rate of new sensations, new ideas, new philosophies. As a result, like Chuck's two-dimensional creature, they felt at an early age that they had seen everything, tried everything — but they were still vaguely unsatisfied. It seems, then, although none of the three youths states it explicitly, that they all arrived at the East by a process of *elimination*. It was the only world still inaccessible and unconquered, a world that, despite its millennia of tradition, was still completely new in their experience.

Thus, in reading their accounts, one senses that they are trying the East, not merely because they are intellectually convinced of its merits, but because they see it as one of the few remaining untested paths, perhaps even the only one that holds real promise. In short, many of the more philosophical youths, and even some of the less intellectual ones, are meditating simply because they see nothing else to do. After twenty or twenty-five years growing up in modern Western society they have discarded all of the other alternatives. Whether they are justified in discarding these alternatives, whether their intellectual conclusions are correct, can of course be debated, but the fact is that they have rea⸱⸱ ⸱⸱⸱ point. They have tired of the plane that they see around then⸱⸱ third dimension, the sphere, the mandala, beckons too strongly to u⸱⸱ ignored.

9/ THE TRANSFORMATION OF THE SELF

Having listened to a number of youths from the many disciplines, we can try to summarize their common assumptions. What theme underlies the Eastern subculture? What is the purpose of these million youths? In a phrase, it is the *transformation of the self.* The process includes three steps: withdrawal, purification, and enlightenment. All three existed in embryonic form in the drug subculture, but all have greatly matured and expanded in the minds of youths on the road East.

The withdrawal theme consists of two elements. First is the belief that "it's not safe just to live here." It is a sense of tangible and intangible poison which must be deliberately avoided, a conscious or unconscious feeling that it is ultimately dangerous to live a conventional life in present-day America. The desire for safety has caused meditators to go to great lengths to disentangle themselves — physically, emotionally, and intellectually — from the web of modern society. A classic expression of it is the song "Wooden Ships": free, naked, happy people floating in safe isolation from the contaminated ruins of the "landmass madness," singing:

> "We are leaving
> You don't need us."

The other half of the withdrawal theme is *the futility of rebellion*, as exemplified by the "Ralph Nader" conversation: the belief that it is foolish to attempt to reform society, and wiser to retreat and concentrate on the self. It is an extension of the belief, so pervasive in this Watergate and Pentagon Papers era, that the common man has no way of knowing what is really going on, and all the more helpless to alter it. Meditators do not attribute world problems to the malevolence of a few powerful men, or overpopulation, or the Bomb; if things were that straightforward, they might be fighting for changes. Instead, they feel that something more fundamental is amiss, perhaps (as the sphere-searchers might say) even an error in our whole cosmology. As a result, they have withdrawn from the political level to the personal. The conversion of Rennie Davis is a dramatic example. Another example is the song, "Revolution," by a group of former Transcendental Meditators, the Beatles:

> Well, you say you want to change institutions
> Well, you better change your minds instead.

Is it a withdrawal or a copout? Many critics of the Eastern movement have called the withdrawal cowardly, even neurotic, as if it were a frank admission of weakness to abandon society in favor of retreat and meditation. And a fair number of meditators, as we heard, have unconsciously accepted that definition, with consequent guilt. For some the withdrawal probably is a copout, and in many cases it may contain neurotic elements: bizarre fears of poison, fantasied dangers, exaggerated feelings of helplessness, or severe anxiety. But most of the meditators I met were not cowards. Their withdrawal was a positive act, a considered decision, a retreat *to* rather than a retreat *from*. Often much courage was required, a willingness to repeatedly say "no" to a thousand subtle or not-so-subtle demands for conformity from parents, schools, and other authorities, in order to begin their new lifestyles.

Not all meditators go so far as to live in communes or farm in the country, but even the more conventional ones have withdrawn intellectually from Western scientific and religious tradition in significant ways. As several quotations have revealed, some of the most highly educated meditators, involved in orthodox and prestigious occupations, hold a multitude of beliefs that sound very bizarre, maybe even schizophrenic, to the skeptical Western ear. Intellectual withdrawal, like physical withdrawal, may of course be motivated by neurotic elements, such as exaggerated fears of science. But it can also represent a positive, bold decision. I did not hesitate to challenge the philosophies of meditators that I met, and many, despite the attack, radiated an impressive confidence that what they had found, in terms of their own development at least, was right.

After withdrawal, the second step of self-transformation follows directly: most meditators feel that they retain a residue of "impurities" from their past lives. These may be perceived or experienced on various levels: as physical poison, as "stress," as vague anxiety, or as intellectual misconceptions from past education. Regardless of their nature, the impurities must be purged, cleansed from the body and mind by the regular practice of a technique or by increasing love of a master. The purification theme is of course fundamental to both Eastern and Western religions, and in a more scientific format, to most schools of psychiatry. The meditators' view is like the psychiatric but even more concrete, in that it extends to physical poisons as well as the mental ones. And many meditators envision their progress in a manner analogous to psychotherapy: elements from the past — poisons, bad emotions, misconceptions — are coaxed to the surface, worked through, and cast off, with a resultant increase in well-being. In addition, like psychoanalysis, many disciplines promise cathartic jumps, moments when impediments suddenly fall away and a new level of purity is attained, as in *satori*, cosmic consciousness, or union with a master.

The task of purification might seem an inevitable corollary of withdrawal, but it is not. The drug subculture, for example, was equally removed from the mainstream of society, but displayed only a trace of the purification theme. The desire for purification, on both physical and mental levels, is one of the distinguishing features of the Eastern subculture. Meditators are unanimously convinced that static withdrawal is not enough; however optimal the new environment, they want an actual program, a technique, to purge past influences.

We have heard a number of examples of the purification theme in earlier chapters, such as the fasting-and-diarrhea conversation, Ellie's account of the Fillmore, or the stories of Fred and Cory. In conclusion, here are two brief final examples of the purification theme. The first is the doctrine of Transcendental Meditation with reference to "stress." Stress is pictured in TM as a semi-quantifiable entity, an almost tangible substance accumulated in various amounts from incidents during the day, but for the ordinary man, disposed of less rapidly than its rate of accumulation. When intake exceeds output for long enough, as it were, toxic levels gradually supervene and result in symptoms of suffering. The array of common methods to cope with the excess stress — aggression, promiscuity, sleeping, drinking alcohol, daydreaming, violent activity, and all the rest — range from moderately inefficient to deleterious. Daily meditation, however, bleeds off the packed stress far more effectively than ordinary activities, and after two to ten years (depending on both one's backlog of stress and devotion to meditation), an entire lifetime's accumulation is purged. Whether or not Transcendental Meditation actually works on this principle may be debated, but the venerable Eastern theory is conspicuously similar to Western psychodynamic formulation of several thousand years later.

A second example is from the lover of Meher Baba quoted at the very beginning of this book:

> "When I first got turned on to Baba, I had this beautiful
> time for the first few months. 'Honeymoon with Baba,' they
> call it. But then I began to come down. I realized that I still
> had selfishness in me. My love for Baba was not complete.
> It was still only a partial love. So then I began to try harder
> to be unselfish and to love Baba, and I started going up again.
> It has gone on like that. Each time I get a little further along.
> I'm slowly working to lose all the selfishness and possessive-
> ness and anger and so on that I've taken on over the last
> eighteen years."

Some meditators are content with merely the first two steps of the transformation process, but the more dedicated youths look ahead to the third: enlightenment. Though they have different names for it and varied methods for achieving it, the great majority of meditators have come to believe that there really exists a higher state of consciousness, a state beyond the bounds of Western knowledge, and perhaps immune to scientific probing forever. As different quotations have shown, many youths have come to believe in enlightenment through experiences with hallucinogens, others by reading books on Eastern philosophy, some by direct contact with a master. And a number of the more sophisticated ones arrived at the same point by gradually rejecting Western scientific and religious beliefs until all of these alternatives had been eliminated. Whatever the origins of their belief in enlightenment, a remarkable number of youths have become so deeply committed to it that they have changed their entire lives, renounced possessions and pleasures, gone to live in communes or ashrams, or even voyaged to the East itself in their quest.

Some youths, no doubt, will eventually become disenchanted with

Eastern philosophy and move on to yet another subculture, much as they left the drug culture a few years before. But many have practiced for five years, seven years, even ten years, and their enthusiasm has not waned. How many of them will ultimately succeed in reaching that higher state, if it exists, is impossible to say. But there is no question of their devotion; the quest for enlightenment has become for them the most important goal, the central task of life.

Here, with the concept of enlightenment, in the domain of Eastern philosophy, this discussion of the Eastern subculture must come to an end. As implied by the teacher of Transcendental Meditation at the very beginning of this book, the answers to the philosophical questions are not verbal, but experiential. This book has made no attempt to reduce them to words. But if the reader, having now heard many voices from the Eastern subculture, wants to experience its philosophy for himself, the techniques and their followers are waiting to receive him.

AFTERWORD: THE METHODS USED IN THIS STUDY

This book is a sequel to my first book, *Voices from the Drug Culture*, for two reasons. First, the recent rise of interest in Eastern disciplines in America has been largely a consequence of the earlier drug scene — in many ways one of its most beneficial consequences. Throughout the pages of this book are many characters similar to those of the first book, in some instances even the same individuals, but now they are several years older and have left the drug world behind.

Secondly, the East has not only followed from the drug scene on a national scale, but in my own life as well. My interest in the East began soon after I first became interested in the drug subculture, in 1966. Over the next few years, that interest slowly grew as I did research for my 1969 college thesis on the subject of drug use. By late 1969, shortly before I started to revise the thesis to make it into a book, I had met a large number of youths who were well acquainted with Eastern techniques. I became sufficiently intrigued, decided to try one, and in December 1969 I was initiated into Transcendental Meditation. I chose TM because it was easily available to me in Boston, because it was systematically taught, and because it did not demand a radical change in lifestyle. I was unable to try a "total environment" technique, such as living in a rural commune, since by that time I was a medical student with all too little time to call my own.

During the next two years, though I personally remained faithful to TM, I gradually began to meet other seekers in a wide spectrum of Eastern disciplines. In general these friendships occurred quite spontaneously, but later, as I conceived the idea of starting a second book about Eastern subculture, I began making contacts and visiting different groups in a more systematic way. During 1972 and 1973, I visited rural communes and urban meetings, tried different forms of yoga, chanting, and meditation, attended courses, subscribed to newspapers, and read innumerable books. All were fascinating, but I learned the most by far from people I met along the way. This book, like its predecessor, is primarily based on the technique of participant-observation, on direct experience with several hundred youths in about twenty Eastern disciplines.

For the skeptical reader, this background will raise several questions. Are my nonquantitative observations really accurate? Did I really meet a "random sample" of youths in the various Eastern disciplines? Am I biased toward TM because it is the technique I happen to practice? What are my biases, anyhow?

To begin with, quantitative data are useful, but almost impossible to obtain in the Eastern subculture. First, it is impossible to locate a true random sample of youths in Eastern disciplines, or even to define what a "random sample" should be in their case. Secondly, even allowing that one could find that hypothetical sample, an accurate statistical work still could not be written. Many youths in Eastern disciplines are too disenchanted with modern society to respond openly to a note-taking interviewer, much less a questionnaire asking them to rate their progress toward cosmic consciousness on a scale of one to ten. Computerized evaluation is exactly the sort of thing they have rejected; few will respond warmly, or honestly, to a researcher who confronts them with anything less than a direct human encounter.

In two cases I performed very circumscribed quantitative studies to answer specific, concrete questions about the Eastern subculture. These have been presented in the first two chapters. But beyond these, the book is based entirely on direct contact with people, many of them good friends. As a result, the book does not aspire to be a precise analysis. Rather I have tried to convey the actual flavor of the subculture and the feelings of its members: their hopes, their fears and angers, their fantasies and beliefs, and the wealth of telling incidents — some serious, some comic — that I encountered along the way. Whenever possible, I have avoided dry description and tried to re-create the quotations, conversations, and scenes as they took place.

The question then arises as to whether my analysis is biased. Can the book really be objective? The answer is that of course it is not objective, nor does it pretend to be. In fact I have at times gone out of my way to clarify my personal sympathies and beliefs. The reasons for this are two-fold. First, as just mentioned, the Eastern subculture cannot be accurately described with objective techniques, however desirable they might be. Secondly, as Rosenthal and others have copiously demonstrated, experimenter bias can distort results obtained under the most rigorous laboratory conditions.* In doing participant-observation work it seems more reasonable for the researcher to explain his personal feelings, allowing the reader to judge for himself the degree of bias.

This leads to several specific remarks. First, although I believe that there probably is such a thing as cosmic consciousness, this book has not attempted to describe or evaluate the actual techniques for attaining it. Many of the techniques are secret, and most are, in some sense, sacred. I would have felt both uncomfortable and unqualified to describe their mechanics in words. Moreover, they are not things to read about second-hand; if the reader wants to decide on their merits, he must try them directly. For these reasons, I have limited this book to the psychological and sociological reasons for the current interest in Eastern disciplines, rather than their philosophical value: the causes rather than the effects of involvement with the East.

Secondly, although I am myself a practitioner of Transcendental Meditation, I have in no way intended this book as an advertisement for TM. In fact, I may have erred on the opposite side and been unduly hard on TM, or at least certain aspects of it. I have no idea whether or not TM is the "best" technique, if such a thing exists, or whether its philosophy is more "right" than any other, whatever that would mean. To be sure, TM is the largest organized group in this country, with a quarter of a million people initiated, and of course I have met more friends over my four years' association with TM than I have from the other disciplines. For these reasons I have drawn a slightly larger portion of my quotations and anecdotes from TM than from other groups. But this probably introduces little distortion in the results, since the TM group is in most ways fairly representative of the Eastern subculture as a whole. In other words, though its members may have a philosophy quite different from

* See R. Rosenthal, "The Social Psychology of the Psychological Experiment," *Amer. Sci.*, 1963, 51: 268.

several of the other Eastern groups, they seem psychologically quite similar.

A final, more personal thought about the question of bias: I suppose every author must have had the curious experience of sitting down to write one opinion and have a quite different one emerge on paper, as if some inaccessible faculty of the mind had already composed what was to be written, oblivious to the more superficial plans of conscious thought. This occurred several times in the course of my writing: I sometimes found myself losing my own arguments, becoming supportive where I had intended to be negative, or turning alternately angry and sympathetic at points where I had meant to remain neutral. Thus the book became a valuable experience in working out my own beliefs, but it emerged as more opinionated than one normally finds in rigorous sociology. Upon rereading it, I decided to let the opinions stand, rather than disguise them with a veil of neutrality; in other words I have not pretended to be value-free. In particular my two fundamental values — a deep faith in science and a belief in the ultimate truth of Eastern philosophy — emerge quite strongly. They may seem contradictory to the reader; he may agree with me on only one or the other. But I believe, now that I have wrestled with them while writing the book, that science and Eastern philosophy are not at all opposed. Only when one or the other is misinterpreted do they seem to clash.

REFERENCE NOTES

CHAPTER 1

Most of the various spiritual movements in this country, along the entire spectrum from the most scientific to the most magical, offer some literature to describe or advertise their techniques. Often this material is not generally available in bookstores, but must be obtained from the groups themselves. The reader who is interested in the literature of a specific spiritual technique, be it Eastern or otherwise, can therefore best begin by seeking out the actual group of practitioners. For general reference, however, the following sources are useful:

Rosenfield, Edward, *The Book of Highs* (New York: Quadrangle, 1973). An excellent source book of contemporary developments in the general area of altered states of consciousness.

Tart, Charles T., ed., *Altered States of Consciousness* (New York: Doubleday, 1972). A fairly technical source book on altered states of consciousness, including many of the areas currently attracting American youth. Extensive and detailed bibliographic material.

The Lama Foundation, *Be Here Now* (New York: Crown, 1971). A very popular recent book introducing many aspects of the Eastern scene. Includes a bibliography of basic works covering many of the Eastern disciplines described in *The Road East:* Zen, several forms of Yoga, Meher Baba, and other masters, etc. The bibliography also includes numerous works by Western interpreters of the East.

CHAPTER 2

For a general introduction to the drug culture in America and the causes of it, see: Pope, H., *Voices from the Drug Culture* (Boston: Beacon Press, 1971). This work contains extensive annotated reference notes covering the medical, psychological, and sociological aspects of drug use.

Hari Dass Baba is quoted in: The Lama Foundation, *Be Here Now* (New York: Crown, 1971), Part III, page 93.

The study of drug use among Transcendental Meditators is: Benson, H., and R. K. Wallace, "Decreased Drug Abuse with Transcendental Meditation — A Study of 1,862 Subjects," in Zarafonetis, C. J., ed., *Proceedings of the International Symposium on Drug Abuse* (Philadelphia: Lea and Febiger, 1970).

CHAPTER 3

On fasting see:

Bragg, P. C., *The Miracle of Fasting* (Health Sciences). Bragg has written many other books similar in form to the above. All are available from Health Sciences.

Wade, C., *The Natural Way to Health Through Controlled Fasting* (New York: Arc Books, 1970).

CHAPTER 4

For an excellent analysis of technocracy in modern times, and the human effects of complexity, artificiality, speed and stress, see:

Roszak, T., *Where the Wasteland Ends* (New York: Doubleday, 1972).

CHAPTER 5

For insightful commentary on growing up in America and the anxiety it may generate, see:

Erikson, E., *Identity: Youth and Crisis* (New York: Norton, 1968).

Keniston, K., *The Uncommitted* (New York: Dell, 1960).

_____, *Youth and Dissent* (New York: Harcourt Brace Jovanovich, 1971).

Roszak, T., *The Making of a Counterculture* (New York: Doubleday, 1969)

Slater, P., *The Pursuit of Loneliness* (Boston: Beacon Press, 1970).

Of these, Roszak is particularly interesting and relevant to the present observations.

CHAPTER 6

The two books cited by Cory, both highly regarded in the Eastern subculture, are:

Lappé, F. M., *Diet for a Small Planet* (New York: Ballantine, 1971).

Nearing, H., and S. Nearing, *Living the Good Life* (New York: Schocken Books, 1970).

The classic analysis of game-playing is: Berne, E., *Games People Play* (New York: Grove Press, 1964)

The story of Nan-ch'üan is taken from: Watts, A. W., *The Way of Zen* (New York: Random House, 1957), page 98.

Lord Krishna's conversation with Arjuna on the battlefield can be read in any translation of the Bhagavad-Gita, such as: Maharishi Mahesh Yogi, *The Bhagavad Gita: A New Translation and Commentary* (Baltimore: Penguin, 1969).

Nietzsche's classic analysis of aggression, asceticism, and morality is: Nietzsche, F., *The Genealogy of Morals,* translated by Walter Kaufmann and R. J. Hollingdale (New York: Random House, 1969).

CHAPTER 7

On the damaging effects of constant change and rapid scientific progress, see: Toffler, Alvin, *Future Shock* (New York: Random House, (1970).

On theta waves, see: Kasamatsu, A., and T. Hirai, "An EEG Study of Zen Meditation," in Tart, *op. cit.* Recent EEG research on Transcendental Meditators, still in progress, has also demonstrated theta waves in advanced meditators. The results, when published, will be obtainable through the Students' International Meditation Society in Los Angeles.

For Jung's essay on flying saucers, see: Jung, C. G., *Flying Saucers: A Modern Myth of Things Seen in the Skies* (New York: Signet, 1969).

Among the recent bestsellers which deal with the mystical are:

Niehardt, John G., *Black Elk Speaks* (New York: Pocket Books 1972).

Bach, Richard, *Jonathan Livingston Seagull* (New York: Macmillan, 1970).

Castaneda, Carlos, *The Teachings of Don Juan: A Yaqui Way of Knowledge* (New York: Simon and Schuster, 1968).

____, *A Separate Reality* (New York: Simon and Schuster, 1971).

____, *Journey to Ixtlan* (New York: Simon and Schuster, 1972).

The Castaneda trilogy is especially interesting, for it parallels the path followed by many youths on the road East. The first and much of the second book center around Castaneda's drug experiences, under the guidance of Don Juan, through which he hopes to become a "man of knowledge." In the third book, however, Castaneda goes beyond drug use, even shuns drugs, in a disciplined search for knowledge. Don Juan changes from the psychedelic guru to something closely resembling an Eastern master.

The books are filled with other themes almost identical to those cultivated among youths in Eastern disciplines: the pursuit of "nonordinary" reality, the emphasis on communion with nature as opposed to the "weakening" influences of modern civilization, and the paramount importance of attaining a long-range spiritual goal under the direction of a master.

On magic in Eastern disciplines, see: Paramahansa Yogananda, *Autobiography of a Yogi* (Los Angeles: Self Realization Fellowship, 1959).

For the study of oxygen consumption among Transcendental Meditators, see: Wallace, R. K., "Physiological Effects of Transcendental Meditation," *Science*, 167:1751 (1970); and the more lengthy monograph of the same title, available from Students' International Meditation Society in Los Angeles.

For commentary on the Western definitions of sanity and insanity, and their flaws, see:

Goffman, E., *Asylums* (Chicago: Aldine, 1961).

Laing, R. D., *The Divided Self* (Baltimore: Penguin, 1965).

———, *The Politics of Experience* (New York: Ballantine, 1967).

Szasz, T. S., *The Myth of Mental Illness* (New York: Hoeber, 1961).

Watts, Alan, *Psychotherapy East and West* (New York: Pantheon, 1961).

On the comparison between psychedelic experiences and Eastern mystical experiences, see:

Clark, W. H., *Chemical Ecstasy: Psychedelic Drugs and Religion* (New York: Sheed and Ward, 1969).

Huxley, A., *The Doors of Perception* and *Heaven and Hell* (New York: Harper and Row, 1954).

Leary, T., R. Metzner and R. Alpert, *The Psychedelic Experience* (New York: University Books, 1964).

Watts, A., *The Joyous Cosmology* (New York: Random House, 1962).

Zaehner, R. D., *Mysticism, Sacred and Profane* (New York: Oxford University Press, 1961).

See also the original book on which *The Psychedelic Experience* is based: Evans-Wentz, W., *The Tibetan Book of the Dead* (London: Oxford University Press, 1960).

The haiku of P'ang Yun, translated by D. T. Suzuki, is quoted in: Watts, A. W., *The Spirit of Zen* (New York: Grove Press, 1958).

On the analogy between the double-bind theory of schizophrenia and Eastern disciplines, see: Bateson, G., *et al.*, "Towards a Theory of Schizophrenia," *Behavioral Science,* 1(4):251(1956), and the discussion in: Watts, Alan, *Psychotherapy East and West* (New York: Ballantine, 1961), pp. 50-54.

The two examples of *Koans* are from: Watts, Alan, *The Spirit of Zen* (New York: Grove Press, 1958), p. 69.

Alpert's account of his guru is from: The Lama Foundation, *Be Here Now,* Part I (New York: Crown, 1971). The Magic Theater appears in the same book, Part II, p. 101.

CHAPTER 9

On the theory of Transcendental Meditation with regard to stress, see: Maharishi Mahesh Yogi, *The Science of Being and the Art of Living* (London: International S. R. N. Publications, 1966).

BIBLIOGRAPHY

The following is a list of works largely in the area of scientific research on Eastern techniques and altered states of consciousness in general. For a sourcebook in this area, see Charles Tart, ed., *Altered States of Consciousness*, already cited. The references and notes in this list have been contributed by Richard Margolin.

Akishige, Y., ed., "Psychological Studies in Zen," *Bull. Fac. Lit. Kyushu U.*, No. 5 and No. 11, Fukuoda, Japan: 1968.

———, Psychological Studies on Zen (Tokyo: Zen Institute of Komazawa Univ., 1970).

Allison, J., "Respiratory Changes During the Practice of the Technique of Transcendental Meditation," *Lancet*, April 1970.

Anand, B., G. China, and B. Singh, "Some Aspects of EEG Studies in Yogis," *EEG Clin. Neurophysiol.,*1961, 13, 452-456. (Also in Tart, C. *Altered States of Consciousness*, 1969 *q.v.*) One of the landmark early studies of the biological effects of practicing an eastern discipline, in this case Yoga.

Barber, T. X., *Marijuana, LSD, Yoga and Hypnosis,* (Chicago: Aldine-Atherton, 1970).

———, *et al.*, eds., *Biofeedback and Self-Control* (Chicago: Aldine-Atherton, 1969) – plus *Reader* (1971). This Annual review of articles, studies, and commentary is the single best source of material regarding the scientific study of altered states and Eastern disciplines.

Dalal, A. S., and T. X. Barber, "Yoga, Yogic Feats, and Hypnosis in the Light of Empirical Research," *Amer. J. Clin. Hypnosis*, 1969, 11, 155-156.

Datey, K., S. Deshmukh, C. Dalvi,and S. Vinekar, "Shavasan: Yogic Exercise in the Management of Hypertension," *Angiology*, 1969, 20, 325-333.

Fisher, R., "A Cartography of the Ecstatic and Meditative States," *Science*, 1971, 4012, 897-904. A survey of the cognitive aspect or experience from the standpoint of the practitioner of meditation.

Goleman, Daniel, "Meditation as Meta-Therapy: Hypotheses toward a Proposed Fifth State of Consciousness," *J. Transpersonal Psychol.*, 3, No. 1, 1971. This article is highly regarded as a discussion of the results of practicing meditation for Westerners.

Green, E., A. M. Green and E. D. Walters, "Voluntary Control of Internal States: Psychological and Physiological," *J. Transpersonal Psychol.*, 1970, 2, 1-26. This is a very important article in the development of biofeedback as a model of the effect of meditation.

_____ , Biofeedback for mind-body self-regulation: healing and creativity. Paper delivered at symposium on "The Varieties of Healing Experience," Cupertino, California, October 1971.

Hoenig, J., "Medical Research on Yoga, " *Confin. Psychiat.*, 11, 69-89, 1968. This is an admirable description of the biological aspects of several yogic exercises, particularly of pranayama (breath control).

Jacobsen, E., *You Must Relax* (New York: McGraw-Hill, 1957). Dr. Jacobsen is a pioneer in the study of relaxation in scientific terms. Relaxation, in many forms, is both a goal and a path for many Eastern disciplines.

Lesh, T., "Zen Meditation and the Development of Empathy in Counselors," *J. Humanistic Psychol.*, 1970, 10, 1, 39-74. One of the few reports of the effect of meditation upon the emotions. Good as background.

Maisel, E., *The Resurrection of the Body* (New York: Delta, 1972). An exposition of the remarkable technique of kinesthetic re-education, introduced by F. M. Alexander to the West. Developed *de novo* by Alexander, the technique nonetheless incorporates many of the essential fruits of yoga and movement disciplines.

Margolin, R., *Is Man a Prisoner of his Senses?* and *Toward a Neuro-scientific Understanding of Consciousness,* two unpublished manuscripts. The author tries to examine one aspect of human experience, the world of the senses, in terms of the latest scientific evidence and the timeless traditional wisdom and to point toward a model of brain functioning which explains this. The claim that ordinary man is in fact a prisoner of his senses is central to many developmental disciplines of both East and West.

Maupin, E. W., "Responses to a Zen Meditation Exercise," *J. Consulting Psychol.*, 1965, 29, 2, 139-145.

Shirota, Jon, "Proving the Power of Meditation," *Probe,* 1970. The only published study to date on Swami Rama, who came to the West only a few years ago with the avowed intention of proving to skeptical researchers what yoga can do.

Tart, C., "Scientific Foundations for the Study of Altered States of Consciousness," *J. Transpersonal Psychol.*, 1971, 3, 2, 93-124.

——, "Transpersonal Potentialities of Deep Hypnosis," *J. Transpersonal Psychol.*, 1970, 2, 1, 27-40.

Wenger, A. M., B. K. Bagchi and B. K. Anand, "Experiments in India on Voluntary Control of the Heart and Pulse," *Circulation,* 1961, 204.

In addition to the books already cited, the following works about specific Eastern disciplines and philosophies are particularly interesting:

Aurobindo, Sri, *The Synthesis of Yoga* (Pondicherry, India: Sri Aurobindo Ashram Press, 1955).

Bennett, J. G., *Dramatic Universe,* 4 vols. (London: Hodder and Stoughton), several printings. Mr. Bennett's writings offer a clear exposition of the writings of G. I. Gurdjieff, of whose teachings he is the best known living exponent.

——, *A Spiritual Psychology* (London: Coombe Springs Press, 1961).

Chogyam Trungpa, *Meditation in Action* (Berkeley: Shambala Press, 1969). The author is the foremost exponent of Tibetan Buddhism in the United States; this book is a succinct guide for anyone wishing to understand meditation as it has been traditionally practiced in the East.

Goleman, Daniel, "The Buddha on Meditation and States of Consciousness: Part I — the Teachings," *J. Transpersonal Psychol.*, 4, No. 1, 1972.

____ , "The Buddha on Meditation and States of Consciousness: Part II — A Typology of Meditation Techniques," *J. Transpersonal Psychol.*. 4, No. 2, 1972. These two articles by Mr. Goleman taken together form an excellent guide to essential Buddhism; that is, Buddhism before revision by later "scholars." The *Visuddhimaga,* an ancient text which is the basis for these articles' discussion, sets forth an exact path through the higher states of consciousness.

Gurdjieff, G. I., *All and Everything, or Beelzebub's Tales to His Grandson* (New York: Dutton, 1950, 1973).

____ , *Meetings with Remarkable Men* (New York: Dutton, 1969). Gurdjieff's writings are neither interpretation of the East nor innovation of the West, but rather spring from that timeless well of wisdom which has sustained mankind's search for meaning in the face of all adversity. The latter book is recommended for newcomers.

Merton, Thomas, *The Way of Chuang Tzu* (New York: New Directions, 1965). A group of stories from Chinese texts illustrative of the state of enlightenment and its independence from the state of rational thought.

Ouspensky, P. D., *In Search of the Miraculous* (New York: Harcourt, Brace, & World, 1949). The record of a personal search through the East for an understanding of the meaning of man's existence.

Suzuki, D. T., *Essays in Zen Buddhism* (First Series) (New York: Grove Press, 1961). This is one of several books about Zen by the man who has done the most to introduce Zen to the English-speaking world.

Thera, Nyonaponika, *The Power of Mindfulness* (San Francisco: Unity Press, 1972). A good introduction to the general type of meditation known as Satipatthana Vipassana, or Mindfulness.

Watts, Alan, *The Book: On the Taboo against Knowing Who You Are* (New York: Collier Books, 1967). Perhaps Watts's most famous book, especially among youthful readers, this expresses the thesis basic to many of his works, namely that modern man has lost the sense of himself as part of nature, and that he regards the world as a set of objects to manipulate rather than as a whole of which he is a part.

———, *This is It and Other Essays* (New York: Collier Books, 1967). Particularly interesting in this is the essay "Beat Zen, Square Zen, and Zen."

For further material, see numerous other books by Merton, Ouspensky, Suzuki, and Watts, as well as books by Eastern masters such as those listed in *Be Here Now*, cited above.

INDEX

Acupuncture: 106-107

Adulthood: coming of and anxiety, 67-83; conception of, 119; fear of aging, 83-87

Advertising, persuasive power: 50-51, 52

Aggression: Eastern philosophy and, 95-97; expressing, 29-30; and meat diet, 69-70; and righteousness, 93-95, 97; and technology, 96

Alcohol, use of: 88, 89, 90

Alpert, Richard. *See* Baba Ram Dass

Amphetamines: 28,43

Ananda Marga: 9-11, 14, 18, 32-33

Anger: Eastern philosophy and, 95-97; expressing, 29-30, 96

Anxiety: coming of adulthood, 67-83; Eastern disciplines as relief from, 29, 67-72, 87, 137; fear of drug arrest, 73-74; fear of organized crime, 75

Arjuna: 96

Artificial, fear of the: 59-61, 62, 65, 90

Asceticism: 97-99

Ashrams: 12, 99-100

Astrology, as spiritual pursuit: 13

Authority figures, concept of uncaring: 52

Autobiography of a Yogi (Yogananda): 114-115, 129

Baba Ram Dass: 12, 30, 42, 101, 122-123, 127, 133

Bateson, G.: 120, 121

Be Here Now (Baba Ram Dass): 101

Belladonna: 117

Benson, H.: 34, 36, 37

Berne, Eric: 93

Bert: 116-117

Bhakti Yoga: 18

Binh, Madame: 4

Black Elk: 113

Brave New World (Huxley): 113

Buddhism: 11; Tibetan, 11, 14, 18. *See also* Nicherin Shoshu

Butch: 60-61

Calvinism: 126

Cancer, self-cure promoted: 106, 115

Change, effect of rapid: 110-111

Childhood, egolessness of: 120

Chogyam Trungpa: 18

Christ: 96

Christianity: 126

Chuck (Transcendental Meditator): 130-132

Chuck (Vermont ashram): 99-100

Clark: 73-74

Cocaine: 22

College life, detached from reality: 80

Communes: 14, 38

Complexity of society, and inability to ascertain risk to self: 52
Conformism, aversion to: 80
Consciousness: 99, 130; states of, 1-3
Contac capsules, overdose: 45-46
"Copping out": 81, 93
Crime, organized: 25-26; fear of, 75

Darwin, Charles: 111
Davis, Adele: 109
Davis, Rennie: 3-6, 136
Death: belief in life after, 125-126; fear of, 83, 86
Diet: 38-41; fasting, 47-48, 98; fruit, 107-108; macrobiotic, 15, 18, 27; meatless, 40-41, 69-70, 89; toxicity of prepared foods, 39-40, 41, 47, 48-52, 60, 90
Diet for a Small Planet (Lappe): 89
Discipline: emphasis on, 61-65; uplifting effect of, 63-64
Divination: 13
DMT: 24, 57
Don Juan: 113
Donovan: 57
Double-bind theory, schizophrenia: 120-123
Drug use: abatement, 22-26, 34-37, 111; Establishment and, 24-25; former, by meditators, 28, 88, 116-117; medical, 109; and organized crime, 25-26, 75; scope, 21; a spiritual pursuit, 13; subculture of sixties, 21, 57; and toxicity perceived, 41-44, 90

Earle: 124-127, 133
Eastern disciplines: emphasis on purity, 39-44, 59, 137; identity value, 31-34; misused, 95-103; philosophical attractions, 124-134; range of, 13-15; scientific investigations, 111-112; size of subculture, 15-20; social attraction, 31; as a subculture, 28-34; substitute for drug use, 30, 34-37; and transformation of the self, 135-139

Eastern philosophies: growth of American interest in, 1-12; prestige accorded age, 84
Education, and drug use: 22-23
Ego, rejected: 116-123
Ellie: 54-57, 127-130, 133, 137
Energy, use of concept: 107, 110
Enlightenment: 130, 138
Entropy, accepting evidence of: 104-105, 109
Erewhon Trading Post: 17
Eric: 100-101
Erikson, Erik: 80
Establishment: factor in waning drug use, 24-25, 111; withdrawal from via Eastern disciplines, 29

Farming: 27, 90-91
Fasting, to purge poisons: 47-48, 98, 137
Fillmore Auditorium, concerts at: 55-57
Fromm, Erich: 97
Fruit, diet of: 107, 109
Futility: 135-136

Ganga Dhar Babu: 114-115
Garden analogy: 112-113
"Grease withdrawal": 40-41
Guilt: 88-92, 96, 100-101, 102-103, 136; sources, 92-93
Gurdjieff, G. I.: 12

Hallucinogens: 22, 28, 30, 36, 117, 138
Hare Krishna: 14, 18
Hari Dass Baba: 21, 30
Harold: 43
Harold (Fred Leonard's roommate): 84
Hashish: 34
Hatha Yoga: 11, 18
Health, concern for: 85-86
Heroin: 22, 26
Hui Neng: 100
Huxley, Aldous: 12, 30, 113, 119, 127, 133

I Ching: 13
Identity: and drug subculture, 26, 31-32; and Eastern disciplines, 31-34
Integral Yoga: 18
Intolerance, among meditators: 32-33

Japanese fencing: 95
Jeff: 104-106
Jefferson Airplane: 57-59
"Jesus freaks": 13, 27
Joe: 75
John: 54-57
Jonathan Livingston Seagull: 113
Judo: 14, 95
Jung, Carl: 113

Karate: 14
Karma Yoga: 63
Keith: 108
Ken: 104-106
Kirpal Singh: 14, 18; ashrams, 14
Koans: 121
Krishna, Lord: 96
Kriya Yoga: 18, 27, 129
Kundalini Yoga: 18

Lahiri Mahasaya: 114-115
Laing, R. D.: 118
Lama Foundation: 42
Leary, Timothy: 12, 30
Leonard, Fred: 67-72, 137
Life after death, belief in: 125-126
Living the Good Life (Nearing and Nearing): 91, 101-102
LSD: 21, 24, 26, 28, 30, 35, 36, 44, 57, 79, 88, 127-130; lack of effect, 122-123; pedomimetic effect, 119-120; toxic effects perceived, 44-47

Macrobiotics: 15, 18, 27
Magic: 13, 27, 114-116; through technology, 114
Maharaj Ji: 3, 4, 5, 11, 12, 14, 16, 18, 20, 28, 33, 47, 87, 106

Maharishi Mahesh Yogi: 13, 20, 57, 112
Marijuana: 22, 24, 28, 34-35, 36, 79, 88
Martial arts: 14-15
Masters and Johnson: 111
Mayer, Jim: 38-41, 45-47, 81
MDA: 74
Meat, abstinence from: 40-41, 69-70, 89; and lowered aggressiveness, 69-70; righteousness of some vegetarians, 94
Medicine, Western criticized: 106-107, 108-110
Meditation, practice of: 2-3, 9-11, 71, 91; and energy, 107; physiological effects, 111, 115
Meditators: 15, ages, 18-20; former drug use, 28, 30, 34-37; intolerance among, 32-33; theta waves of, 111
Meher Baba: 7-8, 11, 14, 15, 18, 27, 87, 98, 129, 138
Mercury, and fish: 49-50
Mescaline: 24, 57
Methaqualone: 75
Miracles: 114-115
Myths, need for: 113

Nan-ch'uan: 95
Nature, trend toward and fear of poisons: 59-61
Nearing, Helen: 91, 101-102
Nearing, Scott: 91, 101-102
Needs, unsatisfied: 112-116
Nicherin Shoshu: 8-9, 11, 14, 16, 18, 43
Nietzsche, Friedrich: 96, 98

Operation Intercept: 22
Ouspensky, P. D.: 12, 129

P'ang Yun: 120
Paramahansa Yogananda: 27, 114, 116, 129
Passivity, and Eastern philosophy: 95-97, 101

Poisons: of drugs, 41,44; environ-
mental, 76; through food addi-
tives, 39-40, 47, 48-52, 60
Pollution, dangers perceived: 42, 47
Polysorbate 80: 50
Practitioners. *See* Meditators
Pranayama, practiced: 6-7
Proof, and scientific method: 104-106
Psilocybin: 24
Psychotherapy, a spiritual pursuit: 13
Purification theme: 39-44, 59, 137
Puritanism: 98, 101, 126-127

Raja Yoga: 18
Ramakrishna: 18
Ramana Maharshi: 18
Randall, Cory: 88-93, 137
Ray: 32-33
Righteousness game: 93-95, 96,
101-102

Samurai: 95
Sanity, concept of: 117-123
Satori: 130, 137
Schizophrenia, double-bind, theory
of: 120-123
Scientific thought, rejected: 29,
104-112
Scientology: 13
Self-Realization Fellowship Hermitage:
27
Self, transformation of: 135-139
Skinner, B. F.: 111
Sleep, orientation effects: 107
"Soul Rush '73": 5-6
Soybeans: 39
Steve: 76-77, 79
Stress, meditators' sensitivity to:
81-83, 137
Students' International Meditation
Society (Cambridge): 68
Subcultures: affluent backgrounds,
61, 80; commercialization, 25;
drugs, 21-37, 111; Eastern disci-
plines as, 28-34; size of Eastern

disciplines, 15-20
Sufism: 18
Sugar, refined/unrefined: 60
Szasz, T. S.: 117, 118

Tai Chi: 14-15, 18
Tantric Yoga: 18
Taoist Meditation: 18
Tarot cards: 13
Technological development: affinity
for, 55-57; aggression and, 96;
complexity, 52, 108; opposition
to, 20, 65-66
Teresa: 63
Theta waves: 111, 120
Tibetan Buddhism: 11, 14, 18
TM. *See* Transcendental Meditation
Tobacco, guilt about prior use: 101
Toffler, Alvin: 110
Transcendental Meditation: 11, 13-14,
81, 98, 115, 137-138; assembly, 1-3;
and reduced drug use, 34-35; size of
following, 16, 17-18
Truth, kinds of: 104-106

Urban life, stress of: 71, 82

Vitamin use: 70, 84-85, 108
Voices from the Drug Culture (Pope):
72, 88-89

Wallace, R. K.: 34, 36, 37, 115
Wall Street Journal: 20
Watts, Alan: 27, 97, 98, 117, 118,
121, 127, 133
Withdrawal: 29, 135-136
"Wooden Ships": 58-59, 135

Yoga: 91, 98; forms of, 11, 14, 18
Youth: defined, 19; as meditators,
18-20; spiritual pursuits of, 13-14

Zen: 11, 12, 18, 27, 32, 95, 98;
communes, 14; *Koans,* 121